for Tammy
with best wishes

HURRICANES
TO
ANTARCTICA

Printed in the United States of America
by New Hanover Printing & Publishing
www.newhanoverprinting.com

Cover Art: *Eye of the Storm* by Frank Loudin
www.frankloudin.com
Cover & Book Design: Kerry Molessa
Interior photos provided by the author or used with permission.

HURRICANES
TO
ANTARCTICA
TALES OF A NAVAL AVIATOR

CAPT. ALFRED N. FOWLER, USN (RET.)

For Katie
September 22, 1926 — April 27, 2012

The wind beneath my wings

CONTENTS

INTRODUCTION

In a ski-equipped C-130 the mission that day was to place a field party out in West Antarctica near the base of the Antarctic Peninsula. I'll never forget it because that was the day, November 13, 1972, we managed to survive a sudden impact; an unintentional hard bounce off the invisible surface of what is called the ice sheet—centuries of accumulated snow—continental in extent and miles in depth.

The summer operating season in Antarctica had just begun; the winter-over team at the U.S. research station at the South Pole had been relieved. Refueling and resupplying the station, perched on two miles of ice at the bottom of the world, was under way. Several major research projects, being resumed or newly installed, had already been flown to the South Pole, and to other remote sites.

Among all the nations operating in the Antarctic region (south of 60° south latitude), the U.S. alone has enjoyed the advantage of long-range, ski-equipped cargo aircraft. The summer operating season is limited to three months; and without such aircraft, access to the interior is only by tractor traverse or by man-hauling, as it was done when man first reached the South Pole one hundred years ago.

There has never been an indigenous population in Antarctica and, thanks to the 1959 Antarctic Treaty, all human activity is limited to peaceful purposes: scientific research and tourism along with the essential life support and logistics.

The age of discovery peaked during the nineteenth century and culminated when first a Norwegian and then a British expedition managed to reach the South Pole during the 1911-12 summer. The U.S. Navy had participated prominently in the discovery age with the Exploring Expedition by Lieutenant Charles Wilkes in 1840, and then, later, by the Admiral Richard E. Byrd expeditions.

The shift from discovery to scientific research occurred in the 1950s.

International scientific cooperation had bloomed after World War II, with special attention being given to the polar regions, the Antarctic in particular. The result was the International Geophysical Year of 1957-58 (IGY), a huge, coordinated effort by twelve nations to study the earth with its ocean, ice and atmosphere components south of 60° south latitude.

The U.S. Antarctic Program was born as part of the IGY. All of the necessary logistics support and expeditionary operations evolved within the Department of Defense (DOD) under the banner of the Navy's Operation Deep Freeze. It flourished for about twenty-five years, with units and personnel from the Marine Corps, Coast Guard and Army as well as the Navy—as Task Force 43 with a rear admiral in command. Then, in 1971, as a result of a forced reduction in the DOD budget, the line item for Task Force 43 was eliminated; management and funding for the U.S. Antarctic program including all logistic support was reassigned to the National Science Foundation.

I knew next to nothing of that background in 1971 when I received orders which, a year later, placed me in command of Task Force 43. The other components, purpose and scope of the operation remained the same, but the admiral's billet, staff and headquarters located in Washington had all been eliminated. And that explains how I, an ordinary captain, happened to be crouching behind the two pilots at that terrifying moment a year later in West Antarctica.

The crew had followed well-established procedures: having found a suitable surface in the required location, they dropped a smoke flare, then dragged the trailing edge of the main skis on a touch-and-go pass, and flew back over it to assess the surface. It would be unacceptable, for example, if a recent storm had left a deep layer of soft powder. A safe landing could be made to happen in that stuff, but a takeoff, without using extreme measures, could not. Two, four or six JATO (jet assisted takeoff) bottles can be attached to the fuselage behind the wings and fired during a takeoff attempt in deep, soft or sticky snow. They burn for about ten seconds and provide additional thrust. Another likely showstopper might be a hard ice surface molded into an unacceptable pattern of waves called *sastrugi*. Then, of course, there is the possibility the plane's ski tracks might reveal otherwise hidden crevassing.

On that day, the surface was OK and the crew, using the smoke flare and the established tracks to know where the surface was, as well as the wind direction, set the bird down gently, not worrying about running out of runway.

The rear ramp was dropped; snowmobiles, cargo sleds, a four-man science party and a ton of food, fuel, tents, equipment and supplies were unloaded. The aircraft was required to remain until the field party had set up their shelter and established radio contact with McMurdo Station. With that done, we boarded the plane, used a rhythmic power surge to unstick the skis, and made a big, sliding circle around the area to line up into the wind in the same tracks made by landing. Without the payload, the takeoff was a piece of cake. The flight deck crew checked all systems in the green while climbing out, and after a few minutes the pilot established a shallow turn and announced we would go back over the field party for an A-OK wave.

At this point, it was obvious that there were no clouds except the high overcast that totally blocked the sun. So, while there was no obstruction to visibility, there also were no shadows, no horizon, no contrast, and absolutely no difference in the sphere of bright whiteness up, down and sideways. The pilot, on instruments, completed his climbing turn, rolled out on the heading to take us back over the camp, leveled and set cruise power. His plan was to get the camp in sight and then let down for a low pass.

Then we struck the surface. Fortunately, the wings were perfectly level and the landing gear with skis was only about half retracted. The aircraft bounced back into the air as full power was applied. The partly folded struts took the brunt of the impact and broke. I scraped my uninjured self off the deck behind the pilots, and realized that we had survived a crash landing situation. Indeed, there were no injuries (except perhaps the pilot's pride in his airmanship) and no damage, except to the landing gear. It wouldn't extend or retract normally. The crew used procedures from their training to do a gravity extension of it to the down and locked position; then chained it, fixed in that position.

We needed to use an emergency refueling camp set up on the Ross Ice Shelf in order to make it back home to McMurdo flying with the gear down. In fact, the next day that plane had to be flown gear down all the way to Christchurch, New Zealand, for repair.

There you have it: my version of probably the most recent of the aviation experiences that I survived. Those stories and other real-life experiences are being offered here to demonstrate why I consider myself to be a very blessed and a very lucky survivor.

Chapter I
The 1930s and 40s

I have only good memories about growing up in Iowa during the Great Depression. In 1929 my parents with Bob, my older brother, and I had moved in with quite a number of other relatives to live at my great aunt's truck farm just outside of Waterloo, Iowa. I didn't realize until I was much older that the whole bunch had just dodged the homelessness bullet. My dad was very fortunate during the Depression to land a job as a Coca-Cola route salesman. His career with Coca-Cola lasted thirty-five years. There were hard times during my grade school years, but we were never poor.

I was, however, confronted by what I thought was a life-threatening experience. When I was nine years old I came down with tonsillitis. The doctor told my mother that I must have an operation. So it was off to the hospital. Early in the preparations my mother must have remembered that in 1926 I had been born at home in my great-grandmother's living room, and accordingly, had not been circumcised.

The ether they used for anesthetic in those days really knocked me out. As I started to come out of it, I knew I wouldn't be able to talk, but fully expected to get some of the ice cream that Bob said they would bring for me. So, I was in fairly good spirits when some white-coated guy came in and told me that I must not attempt to ride a bike for about three months. I was in silent shock; but he left and a big mean nurse came in muttering that she had to change my dressing. Well, my throat was really hurting but I couldn't imagine her changing the dressing on it. You can only guess what happened next. I was trying to defend myself but she was too big and mean. She had me all uncovered and exposed. I was horrified at the sight of it (I could see it then), and the smell!

I couldn't actually yell, but I really needed a policeman. I had been mutilated! The nurse pretty much ignored me and left. I never got the ice cream either. The doctor had been right about the three months' recovery time. I was totally missing from gym class, the swimming pool, etc. for longer than that. But, I survived.

Just before our country entered World War II, my folks, having always lived on the West Side, bought a house on the East Side of Waterloo. I started tenth grade in 1941 at East High School as if I had infiltrated enemy territory.

The attack on Pearl Harbor and the declaration of war against both Germany and Japan changed everything. In just a few months, by the summer of 1942, U.S. mobilization for war was total. All manufacturing was converted to weapons and war material. The John Deere tractor plant in Waterloo started building tank transmissions. The draft of all able-bodied men to serve in the military was well established. Manufactured consumer products disappeared. There were no new tires for private cars. Gasoline, sugar and many food items were rationed. To conserve gas and tires, a nationwide speed limit of 35 miles per hour was set for all highways. People listened to the radio to follow the war news and would see some of it in the newsreels at the movies. More and more men were signed up and shipped out in uniform. My dad, almost forty, tried to enlist but didn't pass the physical. Katie's dad, Ivan Shadle, my future father-in-law, was a veteran of service in the Navy aboard the USS *Arizona* during the early 1920s.

Everyone had a job. The days of the Depression were history. I got a job at Glessner's Phillips 66 filling station on the West Side. I worked after school, Saturdays and long days throughout the summer.

Meanwhile, at East High, a most astounding development was under way. The most beautiful girl, probably in the whole world, but certainly that I had ever seen, was right there. She was Katie Shadle. But it was more than her good looks. She was smart, always smiling and had the kind of charm and outgoing personality that attracted lots of friends, especially boys. In the boy-girl arena I was utterly inexperienced, awkward, shy and inept, but now I was getting motivated.

One of my best friends was Frank Metcalf. He had been taking Katie to the school dances. One was coming up, so he suggested I come along and get acquainted. I did; we did, and I asked her to go to a movie with me. That day we walked from her house downtown, saw the movie and walked back, talking and holding hands all the way.

On her front porch I looked in her eyes, we kissed and WOW! That first kiss generated a reservoir of love, passion and energy to last a lifetime. I was hooked; the shyness was gone. I asked her to go steady with me. She said yes. We said goodnight, until tomorrow. I ran all the way home. There have been sixty-nine years of tomorrows. Since that night in 1943, the rest of our lives has been truly one. It is nothing less than a miracle, and, of course, I consider myself hugely blessed.

We finished high school as an inseparable couple, graduating in 1944. We were deliriously happy, enjoying life together as the war raged on. We watched all of the men of the classes of 1942, '43 and '44 get drafted. My brother, Bob, was called up and went in the Army.

At that time, I had a vague hope that I might somehow get into pilot training. Then in the summer of '43—WHAM! There it was—a poster with the words: "Young men of 17, win your wings of silver." I would be seventeen on August 29. My mother gave her permission and I hitchhiked down to the recruiting station in Des Moines, took and passed the physical and was sworn in as an inactive private in the Army Air Corps.

Among the other men there in Des Moines trying for an Air Corps enlistment was a guy who was short and skinny. Several of the candidates failed the physical exam, but he passed all parts of it except that his weight was about seven pounds below the minimum. He was told he could try again the next day. Some of us who had passed decided we could help him add those missing pounds. The weigh-in was to be first thing in the morning. So, overnight we made sure he ate all he could hold. We woke him up with minimum time to spare, forbid any emptying of bladder or bowels, and forced him to eat bananas. We had bought ten pounds and calculated that without the skins the bananas would assure his weight would reach or exceed the minimum. It did, and he, too, was sworn in, after spending some time in the toilet.

I was extremely happy, thinking that I would be an Air Corps pilot, and as a bonus, the draft board couldn't touch me. Graduation in June of '44 came and went. There were no orders to active duty. I continued to work at Glessner's gas station.

In September Katie enrolled in college at Iowa State Teacher's College (now Northern Iowa University) in Cedar Falls. She moved into a dorm room with three other girls. There were very few, if any, men students there. I would visit her there almost every evening. Mr. Glessner let me use the 1933 Plymouth coupe that he had at the station. I painted it with the Phillips 66 green and orange colors. The 1944 fall turned into winter. Katie and I continued to be the happiest couple on the planet.

My dad had introduced me to Okeh Glessner in 1942, knowing that Okeh would be a wonderful man to work for and learn from. It was my very good fortune that Mr. Glessner hired me to work at his station and tutored me in life, integrity, friendship and in caring for others. I quickly learned what to do when the bell rang indicating a vehicle had driven up to the pumps in one of the service lanes. First, and most important, was a cheerful greeting for the driver with the intent that, if he was not already an old friend, he would soon be one. In addition to satisfying the customer's request, tire pressure including the spare, and all engine fluids, battery included, would be serviced, never forgetting the cleaning of windows.

There were no plastic cards in those days so the purchase of gasoline required both cash and ration stamps. I remember there were three kinds of gas ration stamps: for cars, for trucks and for farmers. I became aware that an illegal market evolved in the improper handling of gas ration stamps. But none of that happened at Glessner's station. Okeh's professional, as well as personal, behavior was strictly by the rules. He set a high standard of decency that rubbed off and has stayed with me ever since.

There are many memories of my days and nights working at Glessner's Phillips 66 station at 2nd and Washington in Waterloo. One in particular must be told. It was Christmas Eve 1944. Okeh had gone home to be with his family; he had left me by myself to keep the station open until, let's say, ten p.m. It was very cold, well below freezing, and much of the sparse business was to add antifreeze. In those days most of it was alcohol-based and would boil away leaving car radiators in danger of freezing on cold nights.

Along about nine-thirty p.m., a big enclosed truck pulled in to buy gas. The driver and another man came inside to warm up and say that their heater had stopped working. I agreed they probably needed a new thermostat, that the station surely had a replacement for sale, but that, being alone, I couldn't do the work to install a new one. They had a long cold night of driving ahead of them so I decided to break the rule of not loaning our tools. I loaned them the use of the wrenches they needed. In the light of one of our service lanes, they backed off the two nuts holding down the thermostat housing, replaced the old thermostat with the new one I sold them, put in a new gasket and tightened the nut on one of the ears of the housing . . . and broke it off!

I remembered there was a welding and metal fabrication shop on the other side of town that advertised: "We fix everything but a broken heart." I looked up the number, called and a gruff male voice said, "Bring it over. I may be able to fix it." The three of us locked up, turned off the lights, piled into whatever I was driving, went through town and found the shop. The proprietor opened up for us and fixed the broken housing. He said, "Merry Christmas" and refused payment.

Back at the station, the men very carefully put their truck back together and with the heater operating got back on the road. They were thankful and happy; for me, it was a very heartwarming outcome on a cold Christmas Eve.

In January 1945, the orders finally arrived. I took the train down to St. Louis and then a bus to the Army base called Jefferson Barracks, Missouri. On reporting for active duty as the most junior private in the Army, I was surprised that they treated me so well. I was issued a set of khaki uniforms including a fore-and-aft cap, and told to get into uniform.

I was to get right to work moving groups of draftees to various buildings for processing. There were three of us on the same assignment. As men who had enlisted and been sworn in, we were part of the Army establishment. I have sad memories of that first day, because many of the draftees were old, infirm or just physically unfit. We knew better than to try to march the draftees in formation; we just tried to herd them down the street at a normal pace. Some of them simply couldn't walk that far. I remember asking one of the stragglers about it. He said his hemorrhoids were killing him and he couldn't walk even the first block. I told him to just stay where he was. My partners and I managed to get most of that first group to their destination. We were immediately told to move another group and so on for the rest of the day. A few days later my processing was complete and a troop train moved hundreds of us to Keesler Field near Biloxi, Mississippi.

Twelve weeks of basic training were made memorable by: close order drill in the pine woods; hot days on the firing range; makeshift wooden barracks with sides that folded up instead of windows; floors, footlockers and bunks kept spotlessly clean; and fallout at four a.m. in boots and raincoats for "short arms" inspection, even though we had never seen the town; never been on liberty.

At the end of the twelve weeks there was no word about moving on; we just started it all over again. Eventually hundreds of us boarded another troop train. The weather was really getting hot, and, like all the buildings at Keesler, the train had no air conditioning. Men were packed into four-high bunks, with no room to move. The train spent days parked on sidings, finally arriving at Luke Field, near Phoenix, Arizona.

By contrast, it was wonderful living in the comparatively luxurious standard barracks and working on the flight line with real airplanes. I was assigned as crew chief for six AT-6 trainers. I was responsible for daily inspections, servicing and cleaning. I loved it. I learned how to do engine checks and was checked out to taxi the planes over to the wash rack and back. I really loved that. I discovered that I could taxi the thing fast enough to get the tail wheel off the ground. I'm very lucky that I didn't try to take off.

What I did do was make friends with a pair of pilots who were scheduled to fly a B-25. There were several types of planes at Luke Field, all engaged in various training activities. The B-25 Mitchell bomber is a twin-engine tricycle gear machine with a bomb bay, the one used by Jimmy Doolittle in '42 to fly off the USS *Hornet* aircraft carrier to bomb Tokyo. My friends took me over to their assigned aircraft, told me to climb down into the Plexiglas bombardier's nose position and enjoy the ride. It was fantastic. We spent about an hour and a half seeing a lot of the Arizona mountains and desert. Then they did wing-overs and various steep banks to put the airplane through its paces. I used my hat for a barf bag.

Another thing that happened when I was stationed at Luke Field was the most exciting—and probably qualifies as the thrill of a lifetime. Katie came to see me and stay awhile. I knew she was smart (she ranked higher than me in the top ten percent of our graduating class), could be very determined when her mind was made up, and very persuasive. But it came as a wonderful surprise when I realized what was happening. She had worked a contact with a sister of a friend to arrange a room in a home being used as a rooming house for single women working in Phoenix. Katie had rounded up enough money for a ticket and she had persuaded her parents to let her make the trip. I was already proud of her for lots of fine qualities, but now there was this demonstration of intelligence, tenacity and courage. I was bursting with pride and anticipation.

Katie's train ride was all sitting up in a coach seat for two and a half days. It was crowded; most of the passengers were in military uniform. Her natural charm and attraction won them over to be friends and protectors. She told how she slept with her head on some guy's shoulder, with no worries about her safety or her valuables that were pinned to her bra. Her valuables included a diamond engagement ring that I had purchased with money saved from my earnings at the filling station.

I was waiting in the Phoenix train station, out on the right track when the train stopped. Not knowing which car, I watched them all until I spotted her—in red, of course—and sprinted to wrap my arms around her. I felt like a whole person again; a feeling that has been repeated many times over the years.

I forget how long Katie stayed in Phoenix. I think it was until I got the word about being transferred. What I do know is that it was a very special and beautiful time. We sat on the rooming house porch in the evening and imagined our future. We both wanted a family (I had said I wanted six) but we were firmly attached to the principle that marriage comes first.

And there was another weighty issue that was a real concern to me. I don't think it bothered her so much. It hadn't really come to her attention. At that time I was certainly no student of national and international affairs. But I definitely was part of and influenced by the scuttlebutt in the barracks. It was June of 1945. The war in Europe had been won by America and her allies. Yet the war in the Pacific involved terrible, hard fought battles with no easy end in sight.

The word was that Japan would never surrender but withdraw to its homeland and defend it to the last man and woman. For America and her allies to bring peace to the Pacific area, Japan must be invaded. Land, air, and sea forces numbering at least a million men would be required. I had no idea what was next for me, but I was certain that I would be among the first in that million.

Ivan Shadle knew a lot about young love, military service and dreams about the future. When he had agreed that Katie, his firstborn, only eighteen years old, was to take the train to Phoenix, he wrote a brief letter to me and sealed it in an envelope with a ten dollar bill. The letter said he and Paula knew that Katie and I were very much in love and were meant for each other. It said that if we decided to marry, they hoped it would be and wanted it to be at home, in Waterloo. Then Ivan said, "Take this money and take Katie to a nice dinner somewhere, and if you decide you can't wait until you come home, then you can get married with our blessings."

Then there was another blessing in my life, one that really counted. Under the orders of President Harry Truman, two atomic bombs were used in August to obliterate two cities in Japan, Hiroshima and Nagasaki. The emperor apologized to the world for treacherously starting the war in the Pacific and ordered his country to accept the unconditional surrender. The war was over!

Along with a contingent of other potential pilot training candidates, I boarded another troop train and wound up at Scott Field, Illinois. Katie used her return trip ticket from Phoenix back to Waterloo. I was assigned to air crew radio operators' school. We were up at four-thirty, classes started at six, with a brief break about eleven, and finished at two p.m. There were classes in basic electronics, and much of the time was spent memorizing and practicing use of the Morse code. I still remember it.

Now, with the war really over, the wheels were turning. There would soon be a wedding. I think it was my company first sergeant who agreed I could be gone the weekend of 7, 8, 9 September 1945. With about seven or eight days to go, the license and other details were being worked out. Katie would wear a beautiful light grey suit that, I learned later, her brother Ivan Junior had bought for her. I hitchhiked to Waterloo.

The wedding was Saturday, in the pastor's study at the First Presbyterian Church in Waterloo. Cake and coffee were served afterward at the Shadle house. Both sets of parents, plus Katie's sister, Marjorie, and her three brothers, Ivan Junior, Jim and Larry attended. My brother Bob wasn't there. He had been injured by shrapnel from a German bullet that killed the man next to him. Bob would return home early in 1946 when he was sufficiently recovered.

Katie's mother, Paula, had packed a trunk with Katie's stuff. The bed sheets and her nightgown were at the bottom. There were layers of home canned fruits and vegetables, a holdover from the way of life during the Depression. Mr. Glessner, my boss at the filling station, had sold me his 1929 Buick touring sedan for twenty-five dollars. I had driven it to haul customers out of the snow during the previous winter, and was confident it would get us down to Bellville, Illinois.

We started out about sundown and we didn't make it out of town before returning for Katie's forgotten coat. There had been a tentative plan to spend the night in a Cedar Rapids Hotel. (Remember, there weren't any motels, rest stops, four-lane highways or cell phones in those days.) But I knew I had to be back at Scott Field on Monday morning, so we pressed on in happy ignorance.

We didn't make it there until Tuesday. I ran the car out of fuel. Even with more fuel it kept stalling out. Days later, I found out it was a serious fuel pump problem. Part of the difficulty with that Buick was that it had no starter. It had to be hand cranked. The spark advance and the choke could be set with levers on the steering wheel, but I discovered that the throttle/accelerator had to be pumped when the engine fired while I was doing the cranking. Pumping the accelerator was Katie's job. After we got settled in our Bellville apartment, I did the cranking each day at about five a.m. Katie was always there in her nightie and slippers to help get the Buick started.

But, back to the wedding night trip—a trip that extended through Sunday, Sunday night and Monday. The engine would die and we would be stranded. Cranking wouldn't work; the only way I could get it going was when someone would give us a push. It was usually the farmers who were out on the highway or in sight of it. We met some wonderful people on that trip. On one occasion the farmer in his tractor gave us a push up to and over the top of a hill, only to see that were stalled again down at the bottom. He chugged on down, and pushed us to the top of the next one. It worked. By Sunday evening the engine of that Buick settled down to steady operation. I was afraid to stop or shut it down, so we pressed on.

I had rented a two-room apartment in Bellville, Illinois. On our arrival, wiped out, we left the sheets and nightgown in the trunk. The next morning we realized that our "furnished" apartment was just barely. There were two straight chairs in the kitchen and one more in the bedroom, otherwise no other place to sit. The icebox drained through a hole in the floor. A bare bulb hung in each room. The bathroom was off a central hall and was shared with others. No one stayed in there very long; it was painted brown throughout including the hanging bulb. Uncle Herb, my mother's brother, and his new bride, Gladys, surprised us with a visit. Some of us sat on the bed.

After being AWOL, I was put on KP for two weeks. Katie found a job right away selling shoes for eighteen dollars a week at the department store in Bellville. My Army pay was thirty-two dollars each month, but I was required to buy a war bond and pay for half of Katie's fifty-dollar monthly family allowance. I waited in the pay line on payday for a five dollar bill. (They said it was for personal health and comfort.) Nevertheless, we were a gloriously happy married couple.

The talk all around Scott Base was no longer about invading Japan. It was about the GI Bill and getting signed up for college. I heard about Parks Air College located not far from Bellville, just south of East St. Louis. As soon as I was confident of being discharged in time, I went over to Parks and applied to start in January '46.

Discharged from the Army in November, we returned to Waterloo and lived in Katie's Grandma Mersch's upstairs at 616 W. 6th Street in Cedar Falls. For about six weeks I worked at the filling station and also the second shift at the Rath Packing Company. Rath's was famous at that time for their Black Hawk meat products, especially bacon. Most everybody in Waterloo worked either at the John Deere tractor plant or at Rath's. My job at Rath's was to haul fatback from the hog cut room to the rendering kilns. It was the kind of job no one else wanted, apparently. I wore rubber boots, gloves and a big rubber apron. Big wheelbarrows were loaded in the refrigerated cut room with four-inch thick strips of fat—maybe three feet long—taken from the backs of hogs.

I pushed the loaded wheelbarrow out of the cut room along a corridor to a very hot room which was at the top of the kilns where the fat was rendered into, I guess, lard. The problem was that over a long period of time a lot of those strips of fatback had fallen off those wheelbarrows. The floor and every other surface in that area was slippery. You could see right into the top of the huge vat where you had to dump the fatback. I worried that somebody could fall in there. I noticed that various Coke bottles, cigar butts, half-eaten lunches and other things were being thrown in. I asked one of the old-timers about it and he said, "Don't worry about it. Everything that goes in and doesn't belong in the end product gets well boiled and filtered out down at the bottom."

In January we travelled back down to East St. Louis to live in a two-room upstairs apartment sharing a bathroom with another Parks couple who rented the rest of the upstairs. The GI Bill provided a living expense stipend and paid for all the costs of college. We were lucky to have that. We couldn't have started without it.

I think that the action taken by the U.S. government during the twentieth century that we can be most proud of was the passage of the GI Bill. It provided the veterans the opportunity to complete a college education and to own their own home. Four million had served in uniform and their prosperity after the war, to say nothing of the baby boom, has defined the century. Now, we have passed a new GI Bill in the twenty-first century. Good for us.

Mr. Oliver Parks was an aging aviation pioneer. The college he had created was complete with an airfield, hangars, a dozen airplanes of different types, dormitories, a library, a landscaped campus, shops for teaching aircraft and engine maintenance, classrooms, labs and so forth. The students were exclusively men. We were required to do a certain number of hours of work maintaining the buildings and grounds, and other chores. Everything went at full speed year-round to complete all three degree programs in two and a half years. The degree options were Aeronautical Engineering, Aviation Maintenance and Aviation Operations.

All Parks graduates were required to have earned a pilot's license and an aircraft and engine mechanic's license. There was no gym or swimming pool, but all the students were encouraged to participate in intramural football and baseball, weather permitting. As I recall there wasn't much time for that. I worked hard and focused on the meteorology major in the Aviation Operations curriculum.

With the coming of summer in 1946, Katie was very pregnant. We were both way too young and inexperienced to be having children. With her common sense and instinct Katie grasped the realities of our situation. But, being a complete dumb head about it, I insisted that she must go to Waterloo where her mother, a familiar local hospital, and family doctor were, in my mind, standing by. She acquiesced. Becky was born in Waterloo on July 26, 1946.

Katie's Great Aunt Margaret was a school teacher all her life and when she retired she had enough money to buy that house at 616 W. 6th Street in Cedar Falls, Iowa, where Grandma and Grandpa Mersch lived with her. She had a bedroom and bath on the first floor. The rest of her life's savings were invested in U.S. postal notes that paid a three percent dividend. When my GI Bill eligibility ran out near the end of 1946, it was a loan from Aunt Margaret that made it possible for us to continue and complete my college degree. The loan was repaid with three percent interest at the rate of a hundred dollars per month after graduation.

In September 1946, while we were living in the two-room apartment in East St. Louis, Katie's mom, along with Jim, six, and Larry, three, took the train down to see us. My classmate at Parks, Keith Deaver, and his wife lived in the other second floor room at Mrs. Deem's. Keith had completely rebuilt a gas-powered scooter and equipped it with a sidecar. Seeing that the two little guys would fit in the sidecar, I proposed that I would take them over to the St. Louis Zoo. So, we set out. The scooter struggled but got us up and over the Eads Bridge. We pressed on through the maze of streetcars, buses and taxis, and made it out to the vicinity of the zoo. Without objection from either of my scared-shitless passengers, I managed to get us back home safely.

Having that apartment in East St. Louis in January 1946 was essential to the launching of our life together; a life already foreseen in our dreams to include a family and a prosperous career based on a college education. But by the end of the summer of '46 with baby Becky moving out of a bassinet into a crib, we needed a better place to live.

Gordon Schmal, my classmate at Parks, and his wife, Mary, with Molly, their newborn first baby, were facing the same problem. Mary and Gordon found a small bungalow to rent. It was in the village of Maplewood Park just adjacent to the Parks College campus. In that same village an empty lot was being set up to provide space for four house trailers. One space was still available. We grabbed it. The 19-foot trailer that we bought with Aunt Margaret's loan was parked there and we moved in.

The back end of the trailer was the bedroom. The double bed had been removed and replaced by a crib. A second crib was added in 1948. Katie could barely squeeze into the space between those two cribs. At the other end was a tilt-back couch. When opened it would sleep two. It couldn't be opened unless the table was folded up to cover the corner cabinet.

Our trailer, like the other three, had no toilet or shower. The owner of the lot lived in the house next door and offered the ladies the use of the shower in her bathroom. The men used the showers at the college. Sharing the use of our landlady's laundry equipment was a bit more difficult. She had a wringer washer in the basement. The wet clothes had to be hung on the clothesline. There was no drain down there. All of the water from the washer and the rinse tub had to be thrown by the bucketful out the basement window.

Katie and I necessarily became good friends with the other three couples that lived in our trailer park. The men were Parks classmates. We all shared the outhouse privy. Katie called it "the facilities." There were no lights out there. The use of a flashlight after dark was important in order to minimize awkward scheduling conflicts. Katie had bought a porcelain potty that baby Becky was being trained to use. I came to realize that some of the adults in our trailer park were probably using thunder mugs.

The final eighteen months of college without the help of the GI Bill loomed as a serious crisis for our little family. I had been searching for a part-time job. I tried all day Saturday at Sears, but one of the five dollars earned went for union dues. After several other false starts, I joined up with another married classmate who had a car. With that, we took jobs as curb hops at a big dairy store called Peveley's in Clayton, Missouri, on the other side of St. Louis. The customers parked in big circles facing a colorful fountain. The sundaes, sodas and milkshakes were each a quarter. If you really hustled, you could make a lot of tips. I worked there right up until May of 1948. After my classmate's car died, I began using public transportation to get to work. In the late afternoon it was a local bus to East St. Louis, then another bus that crossed the Eads Bridge, then a short walk to the start of the Olive Street Trolley. I took that westward to the end of the line, and then another bus to the dairy store. To get home, the last bus was at midnight from the store to the end of the streetcar line, in downtown St. Louis. I walked to the interstate bus terminal, caught a bus that went south down the Illinois side of the river, and asked the driver to drop me adjacent to the college. With the income from the tips that I brought home Katie was able to sustain the family.

My private pilot's license at Parks had been completed by way of thirty hours in an Ercoupe. At $7.50 per hour, the first six hours in 1946 were paid for by the GI Bill; the final twenty-four hours were finished in 1948 at our expense.

Oliver Parks had decided to retire. He gave his college, complete with airfield, campus, faculty, staff and students to the St. Louis University. The transition was seamless except we noticed that some of our classes were things like ethics, and taught by Jesuit priests.

Then, with the advance of springtime in 1948, Katie and I were confronted with additional life-changing situations. For one thing, a second pregnancy was well under way. Moreover, all my job applications had been sent to the few airlines that existed then and had been rejected or ignored. With my degree I would be qualified for a job as an airline dispatcher, because of my training in meteorology and airline operations.

But WHAM! The U.S. Navy announced that, because nearly all of the WWII naval aviators had bailed out and the pipeline of trainees had been shut down for a while, there was an urgent need for prospective pilot candidates. The need was so urgent that one of the sources to be drawn on was men who could pass the physical, were no older than twenty-five, who agree to enter Navy flight training, *and* who were recent college graduates. Wow! The best nibble I had from the airlines was an offer to start with Braniff for $97 per month. Ensign's pay with flight pay would be $379, and, what's more, it would be a USN commission by direct procurement.

Things were happening at a frantic pace during the second half of May 1948. Katie's due date and my graduation were both to be 1 June. Our trailer with most of our belongings could stay there for now on that lady's lot near Parks College. The man at the company that sold us the trailer was telling me that, when the time came, he could provide a Cadillac sedan that would handle all of us and pull the trailer down to Pensacola.

So, I took Katie with little Becky back to Waterloo. Tom was born on 30 May 1948. Our childbirth experience followed the same pattern as two years earlier. Katie's doctor once again assured us it would be OK to have our babies in East St. Louis as Katie was both strong and capable. But I was too young and timid. In my mind, it was essential that she be close to her mother when the delivery time was near, just as in '46. Katie accepted it, but she didn't like it. After I had seen Tom in the hospital nursery I joined up with my folks. My dad drove my mother, my brother, and me down to St. Louis. The St. Louis University graduation, including the big class from Parks College, was held in the gym, and then we returned to Waterloo. When Katie and baby Tom left the hospital we stayed with Katie's folks.

When my orders arrived, I was sworn in as Ensign, USN, and was to report on 1 September 1948 at Naval Air Station Pensacola. My maternal grandmother, Grace, who was driving south to see a friend in Texas, agreed to take me and my family down to East St. Louis.

I had a wonderful wife, a two-year-old daughter, a two-month-old son, a house trailer, no car and a set of orders to Pensacola. What could go wrong?

The man at the trailer company said his Cadillac was broke and all he had was a pickup, covered in back. Katie said, "No way, that's crazy." Then we looked at each other for four seconds and said, "Let's do it!"

A tropical storm had come up from the Gulf and it rained for two days. The guy had moving van comforters in the back of the pickup. The cover kept the rain out. There was a canvas flap over the back. Katie and I took turns riding back there. There were no interstates and he couldn't go very fast anyway with that trailer in tow.

Down through Cairo, Illinois, we were doing OK. We would stop in little towns to warm Tom's milk. The used diapers, although normally laundered, were just thrown out. Then, at separate times, both trailer wheels broke. The wheel broke right across the lug bolt holes. The man had sold us the trailer, so he found a way to replace both wheels. Then, about eight hours later, the hub of his fan that draws air through the radiator in his truck failed. He got that fixed, too.

We arrived safely, running low on diapers, at Pensacola, and found a trailer park. We gave the guy with the pickup nearly all of our money and he left. The next day I took a bus downtown, found the store that sells Navy officer's uniforms, and got outfitted with the essentials. They looked at my orders and put it all on an open account. Then I put on the uniform, took the bus to the main gate and reported for duty. It was 1 September 1948. I had been twenty-two years old for all of three days. Katie, as always, was totally resourceful, confident and capable. We were blissfully in love, our dreams of family had come true and the doors of opportunity were wide open.

There were weeks of Pre-Flight ground school. Then my class moved out to Whiting Field. The commuting was by Navy bus for those officers, like me, without a car. I was to fly the SNJ, a single-engine, low-wing monoplane with a tail wheel, the exact same plane as the AT-6 that I had worked with at Luke. My first flight was on 9 December 1948. After a total of nineteen hours I soloed on 28 February 1949. There were many stages during basic pilot training—such as formation flying, instrument flying, gunnery, cross country and aerobatics—conducted at several different outlying airfields.

When I went through Navy flight training, water survival was taught with a very special machine, designed specifically to duplicate the situation when a single engine aircraft went down in the ocean or any other body of water. The aircraft with all its engine weight up front would, nearly always, flip forward and wind up on its back. The survival training mechanism was called the Dilbert Dunker. It was a fuselage mockup, about twenty feet long, with a cockpit just like that of the SNJ, without the glass enclosure, mounted on a rail and set at a steep angle aimed into the deep end of a swimming pool. The student would sit in the cockpit with his shoulder harness and seat belt fastened. Two rescue swimmers would be waiting in the water. When released, the Dunker would go plummeting down the rail, crash into the water and immediately flip upside down. The victim, as he had been trained, would hold his breath, wait until the motion of his "airplane" had stopped, release his seat belt and shoulder harness, push himself downward to clear the wreckage, and swim away until clear and then up to the surface.

As I was preparing for my turn in the Dilbert Dunker, I remembered how Bob and I had used the Cedar River for our swimming pool. For two or three summers in the late 1930s we lived right by the river on W. 10th Street. We were in the water all summer and became pretty good swimmers, so for me, the Dilbert Dunker was lots of fun. Unfortunately, for many of the students it was scary, and for some so frightening that they couldn't take it and were given extra training in the pool. Some of the student aviators that I knew disappeared during formation, gunnery or the aerobatics part of our flight training. I heard that one or two were washed out because of the Dilbert Dunker. I loved the formation flying and aerobatics, feeling very comfortable knowing what the plane could and could not do, and that it would respond exactly the way I was controlling it. Navy flight training, as it was conducted right after the war, was relentlessly demanding. The washout rate was substantial, but I was a survivor.

There continued to be ground school classes and there were weather delays. In the early spring of '49 Katie and I wanted to get out of that 19-foot trailer. There was no market to sell it, but a guy offered to trade it even for a 1941 Oldsmobile. We did it and moved out to a cottage on Perdido Bay, west of Pensacola. The other married officers living out there invited me to join their carpool. I knew there were problems with that Oldsmobile, but it seemed OK. It turned out to have a cracked block and ran rough. When it was my turn to drive, they refused to ride with me.

In those days all naval aviators had to be qualified in carrier landings. That was the final stage of basic. So in June of '49, I delivered Katie with Becky and Tom up to her folks in Waterloo for a visit. I had just found out that I was to be transferred to NAS Corpus Christi for advanced training. Ivan and Paula decided to make a driving trip, taking Katie, Becky and Tom along, to end up in Corpus Christi. I had traded in the Oldsmobile for a 1948 Plymouth sedan. I would be able to drive over to Corpus after finishing carrier quals.

The day came when I was to fly my SNJ in formation with three others to the carrier, the USS *Cabot*, about fifty miles out in the Gulf. The deck of the carrier has three arresting cables across the landing area aft. Then, a ways forward, there is a big, ten-foot high foldable barrier made of cables, so that forward of that there may be other parked airplanes. Angled deck carriers came later.

In the perfect carrier landing, your tail hook catches the second, or middle, wire; you come to a screeching halt, the flight deck crew disengages the tail hook and locks it in the retracted position, the barrier is folded down, and in the case of repetitive qualification landings, the flight deck forward is clear; you crank up full power and take off, go around and do it again.

I felt great doing five of those landings and takeoffs. On the sixth landing my hook bounced over the No. 2 wire, caught the No. 3 wire, and, as the plane came to its sudden stop, the prop nicked the barrier! I was told to shut down, turn the plane over to the deck crew, climb down and report to the air boss.

I was very unhappy and worried. About two days later I went before a student aviator disposition board. With very little deliberation, they sent me back for another sequence of field carrier landing practice, and, if satisfactory, I would do the carrier quals again. What a relief. It was on 30 August 1949 when I finally did my six carrier landings without incident. I had completed basic training with a total of two hundred and ten flight hours.

Ivan and Paula had helped Katie find a furnished house in Corpus Christi, rent it, and move in with Becky and Tom. The owner of that house had advertised that he would accept only renters without kids. It was a nice house, well furnished, and Katie made it clear that she really wanted to live there. When the owner saw Ivan's Masonic ring, an agreement was quickly reached with a handshake. Katie's parents continued on their trip, and she and the kids settled in. She made contact with some of my basic training classmates who had already arrived at Corpus. They helped with transportation for grocery shopping and so on. When I arrived there, it was wonderful having our family reunited, and with a reliable car for transportation. September and part of October were devoted to ground school learning the design, function and operation of systems in the PB4Y-2 Privateer, a four-engine patrol bomber.

Let me explain the Navy's way of designating aircraft types in those days. The first letter identified the machine's function or purpose; F for fighter, A for attack, R for transport. PB meant a dual-purpose patrol bomber. The next letter identified the manufacturer: Y was Consolidated, V was Lockheed, Q was Fairchild, etc. If a manufacturer had developed more than one aircraft intended for the same purpose, then a corresponding number appeared between the letters. Finally, the number of a major modification of a specific plane was added with a dash at the end.

The Privateer, PB4Y-2, was the Navy's application of the B-24 bomber. With a big single tail, it was the dash two; the original twin tail version was the dash one. There is a famous, and rather humorous, unintended consequence of this aircraft designation system. The second modification of the fourth transport aircraft built by Fairchild is forever identified as the R4Q-2!

The decade of the 1940s was finished in style for Katie and me along with Becky and Tom, as on November 23, 1949, I completed Advanced Training. I had flown about a hundred hours in the PB4Y-2 as copilot and navigator. Katie pinned on my Naval Aviator's gold wings. We loaded the car and drove to Iowa to show off the kids and take a break.

CHAPTER II
THE 1950S

I had made a written request that I be assigned, as my first squadron tour, to the Navy Hurricane Hunter Squadron in the Atlantic. I had heard there was another such squadron flying in the Pacific, maybe out of Guam. Luck was with us again; I had orders to report to VP-23 home-ported at the Naval Air Station, Miami, Florida. There was to be intermediate aviation electronics training at Norfolk.

As of January 1950, airborne electronics systems were developing rapidly, but still in their infancy. At the Norfolk Naval Base, I learned about LORAN, RADAR and the latest in radio communications. At the end of February, we finished there and drove down to Miami. We reported for duty at VP-23, got on the waiting list for Navy housing and found a furnished shotgun duplex to rent.

When I think about our time in that house, it stands out as a good example of the challenges confronting the young Navy wife, especially one with small children, who doesn't drive, and must deal with frequent moves while trying to sustain a home. For one thing, it was hot and sultry living in that house. In fact, there was never any air conditioning in any of the hot, humid places in Pensacola, Corpus and now Miami. As it happened, we didn't experience any air conditioning until we moved to a new house in New Orleans in 1957.

NAS Miami in 1950 was a Naval Reserve Air Station located in the northwest suburb of Opa Locka. We called it Masters Field. I don't remember that there were any Naval Reserve air units operating there, but it was home to VP-23 and also the Navy Hurricane Weather Center. It was a small field with just one hangar and 5,000-foot runways. All the other buildings were temporary WWII construction.

In March of 1950 I had to be one of the greenest of green junior officers reporting for duty with the fleet operating units of the U.S. Navy. Even so, I wasn't the most junior; there were several Aviation Midshipmen wearing wings already in VP-23. One of them was "Buster" Nigel. Having met him in Norfolk, Katie and I invited him to ride with us down to Miami. Buster must have grown up in rural Kentucky. He frequently used expressions involving mules, as if they were members of the family, such as, "Don't worry about the mule, just load the wagon," or, "Well, I'll be a suck-egg mule!" But, I digress.

I remember that it was my first day of sea duty and, having just reported in, one of the officers told me I was to be the Education Officer. Before long, someone showed me to that office and introduced me to the Lt (JG)— lieutenant junior grade—that I was to replace. He seemed very happy to see me, wished me good luck and left. As I got acquainted with the yeoman striker assigned there, I was curious to know what went on there and why it was called "education." He seemed pleased to explain it to me.

All the enlisted men in Naval Aviation are matched up with a technical or administrative skill or specialty, each with established steps for advancement in knowledge, experience and pay grade. There were service-wide examinations that the men studied for to establish their qualifications for advancement. My job as Education Officer was to oversee, prepare for and administer the exams.

I was struck then, and even more so now, to realize the very close parallel in the challenges I faced and those confronting the young airmen who were also starting out in the squadron. Primarily, I was faced with a very complex and lengthy flight training process leading to qualifications as Patrol Plane Commander. I was to do lots of flying and it would require more than a year.

VP-23 was a large squadron. There were at least seventy-five officers and just over two hundred enlisted members. We flew and maintained twelve of the big four-engine PB4Y-2 Privateers. The engines were Pratt and Whitney R-2800s swinging three-bladed props. The PB4Y-1 was the Navy's version of the famous WWII Liberator with twin tails. Our 'Y-2s' were virtually the same aircraft with a really tall single vertical stabilizer and rudder. Just like the old Liberator, our planes had six gun turrets, each with twin .50-caliber machine guns: one in the nose, one in the tail, two top turrets and two in the sides of the aft end of the fuselage. The two top turrets were being removed to provide more interior work space.

Each of our twelve air crews consisted of ten to twelve members with four or five officers as the pilots and navigators. The enlisted crew included engineers, radio operators and ordnancemen headed by a crew chief, typically a Chief Aviation Machinist's Mate.

All those guns and turrets gradually disappeared in a few years, but during my training in 1950 and '51 all the flight crew members were required to operate the turrets and fire the guns. There was a live firing range called "Chicken Rocks" at the northwest end of the Bahamas. Many flights were devoted to circling over the rocks as the different crew members blazed away, taking turns in the various turrets. It was more than sixty years ago but I can still remember focusing on those rocks and feeling the surprising power of those guns. Also in my memory is how the pilots would make some pretty low passes and there was talk about the unrealized hazard of rounds ricocheting off the rocks.

In 1950 the use of the guns in defense of enemy fighters was no longer realistic, but using the guns as a potential weapon against a surfaced or snorkeling submarine made sense. Similarly, we didn't train for bombing missions but a squadron of Privateers with the large bomb bays had the capability to lay a minefield at long range.

And we practiced that. I remember being in the left seat one long, dark night. The training mission was for a formation of our planes to lay a minefield in Guantánamo Bay, Cuba, under the cover of darkness. Four planes formed up over the Atlantic and flew for about three hours in radio silence and no running lights, only showing blue formation lights on the wing trailing edge. The procedure calls for the flight to stay in loose formation en route and to close up very tight for the drop. I was on the right wing of the leader. It was a clear night above a hazy broken undercast which meant no horizon and nothing visible on the surface. I was in the left seat. After about two hours of staring at those blue lights on the other plane I realized I was experiencing vertigo. I told the right seat pilot to be ready to take control, because my up-and-down sense of reference while looking out the window had gone all crazy. He flew a while and we were OK through the rest of the mission. I learned from that.

In VP-23 we used the Gulf of Mexico for extended over-ocean navigation training. We would fly long triangle or box patterns at night, departing before the reserve air station shut down and returning just after seven a.m. when they opened. We practiced celestial navigation which was essential before the age of satellites.

During the wee hours on one of those overnighters I was in the copilot's seat. The pilot had the plane on autopilot. I found myself looking out at the stars mostly, but when I noticed that the pilot was dozing I remember being struck with the shocking reality that (a) everyone but me was asleep, and (b) the plane was slowly losing altitude. I punched the pilot and started a lively chatter on the intercom. For me and the various crews I flew with in the future that frightening experience was never repeated.

Navy family housing had been built in the town of Opa Locka. After a couple of months we were able to move into one of those houses, at 946 Superior Street. Each house was unfurnished, a cinder block square with two bedrooms, a bath, living room and kitchen. There was a kerosene space heater in the central hall. Katie used all her magical abilities to find furniture we could afford to furnish the place. (Fortunately we had finished paying off the loan from Aunt Margaret.) We were very happy there for two years.

There are a bunch of memories that come roaring back from our time during 1950 and '51 in Miami. The one that is most profound occurred the night of Tuesday, October 17, 1950. A hurricane had moved north from the Caribbean and crossed Eastern Cuba. It was reorganizing and gaining strength in the Florida Straits. It had no name. Our skipper, Commander Lew Tamny, said he knew all about these things and he decided the path of the beast would stay offshore, going north-northeast. He further decided that the squadron planes were *not* to be evacuated! He predicted the only strong winds would be from the northeast. So, the order was given to park ten PB4Y-2s on a taxiway that had embedded tie-down lugs.

To fit them all in, the planes were pointed to the northeast and parked with overlapping wings. Double tie-downs with quarter-inch cables were placed at both wings, all three landing gear wheels and tail. The engine air intakes were covered and the props feathered to prevent turning in a strong wind. A watch schedule was set for one pilot and one other crew member to be in each aircraft on a four-hour rotation. I had the midnight to four a.m. watch in the skipper's airplane.

I went home to be sure Katie, Becky and Tom were hunkered down. Supper was finished and I went back to the squadron. The wind from the east-northeast was picking up. At about eleven p.m. the radioman in our crew and I went to our plane, relieved the others and looked over the preparations. There were linemen standing by with wands and flashlights. I remember that the taxiway lights were not on. Of course, it was a reserve air station; they always shut down before midnight. The mechanical control lock on our aircraft was set, as was normal when parked. Our radios were on but we were listening only to the other watch crews chattering on our squadron frequency.

In subsequent analysis it was shown that the eye of the hurricane actually moved directly over where we were. What I saw and felt was that the northeast wind increased to gale force and more. I didn't get a reading from the air speed indicator because the Pitot tube was covered, as it usually was when parked. It certainly felt like we were up to lift-off air speed, well over 100 knots.

Suddenly the wind dropped. Someone was yelling on the radio: "We're in the eye! We have to turn around." I certainly understood that. I told my watch mate that I was going to get at least engines No. 1 and No. 4 started in order to pivot around. I sent him outside to uncover all of the air intakes and help the linemen remove the chocks and tie-downs.

Our position on the taxiway was number three from the front of the line. Only the No. 1 guy had room to do a 180. It could only be done in sequence. There was not enough room for any other plane in the line to pivot around. It was a taxiway, for heaven's sake. Why in the world weren't we all scattered out on the runway?

Almost ten minutes had gone by. The No. 1 plane in line was revved up; signal wands were waving. He moved, turned and went around.

I was getting the all-clear to start engines; followed the check list from memory and proceeded from habit to start all four engines. More minutes had gone by. All the voices on our radio channel were climbing in volume and pitch. My memory is clear that the following events happened; I'm not sure about the sequence:

- A big gust of wind slammed us from behind.
- My radioman helper was back in the copilot's seat.
- The heavy gales and driving rain built up rapidly from directly astern.

- I caught sight of the figure of a man (I thought a lineman) get blown off his feet and disappear.
- The radioman yelled that the chocks were out, all tie-downs removed—I was clear to turn.
- I could see that the No. 2 plane had not yet moved.
- Something that looked like part or all of an aileron went sailing by.
- With all four engines running I engaged the autopilot to lock the controls.

At that point the mechanical control lock broke and immediately the hydraulics involved with the autopilot also failed. The yoke was slamming back and forward with powerful force. As I strained to control that, and also to do something about the loose rudder, my seat broke and dropped to the floor. My face was now level with the back stroke of the yoke. I remember that the smell of hydraulic fluid was strong. I was beginning to worry. The radioman valiantly wrapped himself around the copilot's yoke. The full fury of the back side of the storm was on us. All the control surfaces, aileron, rudder and elevators became jammed past the stops one way or the other, or had, most likely, already been blown away. The violence in the cockpit diminished. The radioman got out of the good right seat so I could be there and resume control of the brake pedals.

Our situation was stable; the wreckage of the control surfaces was already done. Nothing further happened for a few minutes. I considered shutting down, but hesitated. I saw the No. 2 plane move a little; then it rapidly weather-cocked 180 degrees to face the wind. A brave lineman with a bright light motioned for me to turn. There was horizontal rain but my partner could see that the piece of taxiway immediately to our left was clear. I released the brakes, locked the left one hard and we spun around. I set the parking brake, shut down the engines and we waited out the rest of the storm.

Nine aircraft were severely damaged with the loss of their control surfaces. The only human casualty was a broken arm as a man tried to close the door of the barracks just as the back side of the storm had hit.

Chief Crissey was the Plane Captain (flight engineer) of the skipper's crew in VP-23. As a junior ensign in the squadron I was very lucky to be assigned as second navigator in that crew. Chief Crissey took me under his wing, taught me a lot about the aircraft, its proper operation and maintenance, as well as a lot about leadership in the Navy. As I progressed as a member of the crew and occupied the right seat more often, I would ask the crew chief for a cup of coffee. Chief Crissey told me that Navy coffee was taken black with no cream, no sugar. After trying that, I didn't like it, so the next time I asked again for a bit of cream and sugar. He satisfied my request with a cheery smile, once or twice, but after that I noticed that my coffee tasted like it had salt in it instead of sugar. That was a simple mistake, since they look alike. Then it was a problem with a can of condensed milk having been left open in the plane overnight. So, for the last sixty-four years I have insisted on having my coffee the Navy way: no cream and no sugar.

I thought about Chief Crissey years later. I think it was when Admiral Elmo Zumwalt was Chief of Naval Operations. Orders came down through Navy channels to support a program called "Moral Leadership." Everyone asked, "What's that?" and "How do you teach it?" The answer turned out that it was simply to set a decent example. That was exactly what Crissey did.

When the manuscript for this story was in its early stages it had been given the title *Decency in Leadership and Life*. There were other false starts, but with the help of my kids and their spouses, the existing title was finalized. But now, while enduring the long wait for publication, I realize that I have more to say about decency in leadership and life.

In my experience there are two ways (which also apply more broadly to the personal relations of life) to approach the manifestation of leadership: one is with decency, caring and firmness; the other is with egocentric, hard-ass meanness. Both approaches can produce desired results, especially in the short term. In the longer view, effective leadership requires the establishing of discipline and teamwork. I believe that teamwork evolves from discipline, which in turn is the direct outgrowth of decency. A leader in any given situation, while attending to the abilities and teamwork of his or her coworkers and subordinates, must also be attuned to their welfare. The leader must reflect genuine caring and set a decent example.

At this point it is important to interrupt the timeline of my story. You twenty-first century readers must understand why our country needed to have Navy Hurricane Hunters in the 1950s. Populations along the Atlantic seaboard and the Gulf Coast clearly need to be warned about the existence and approach of tropical storms and hurricanes. Prior to the 1960s, before there were any satellites, there was such sparse information, as from ship and island reports, that forecast centers were simply unable to issue the warnings that are routine today. There were historic disasters, such as at Galveston in 1900 and the Florida Keys in 1935, where the unprepared victims were trapped before they could evacuate. Yet these huge, counterclockwise, whirling disturbances lumber along across the ocean in a way that the eventual threat to coastal areas can be known many days or even a week in advance. It's not like a tornado that comes out of the thunderstorm and bears down on you in minutes, or even like a tsunami that is triggered by an earthquake on the other side of an ocean area and races across at very high but predictable speed.

During World War II the U.S. Navy lost ships and took a lot of other damage from a typhoon in the Pacific. (The same phenomenon is called a *hurricane* in the Caribbean and Atlantic.) The admirals and ship captains actually did not know enough about the size, shape, location and movement of the thing that might be coming at them.

The Navy understood the potential and, having the resources, decided to develop aerial reconnaissance that could determine the existence, location and general behavior of a typhoon. It came to pass, and by 1948 there was a squadron of patrol planes with that mission at Guam in the Pacific and another at Miami in the Atlantic. That was VP-23.

There had to be a period of gaining experience in how big airplanes could effectively accomplish the discovery, measuring and tracking of tropical storms. The analogy of the beast is that of a huge doughnut of thunderstorms, churning counterclockwise (in the Northern Hemisphere) with spiral bands extending out and a calm, cloudless eye in the center.

Airplane drivers have always known that you don't deliberately fly at normal cruising levels into a thunderstorm. You might be able to fly around it or maybe get up to 35,000 or 40,000 feet and fly over it. The extreme violence and energy of a thunderstorm is associated with the vertical convective currents, like high-speed elevators. This is also the source of the heavy rain, hail and lightning. The process is that of an engine generating vast kinetic energy drawn from the heat of the sunbaked earth or the tropical ocean.

The vertically oscillating blasts of air extend upward to great heights, but downward they are limited by the floor of the atmosphere, the sea surface. Consequently, the best way to fly into and through the rough part of a hurricane is in the lower 1,000 feet above the ocean. I say "best" because it was our experience that in some cases the storm structure was not well organized. Sometimes the open avenue between outer spiral bands can be followed all the way to the eye. If you are dealing with such a weaker storm you may be able to easily reach a position, let's say, 8,000 or 10,000 feet above the point that may appear to be the center of the circulation, and therefore, the location of the storm. But, where exactly are you?

That brings up the next point: navigation. In the 1950s there was no GPS, and there were no satellites or other advanced radar and communication gadgets. Air navigation over the ocean required dead reckoning (DR). I think that word is properly spelled d-e-d, for *deduced*, but is customarily written as *dead*. Position fixes can be established by celestial means; that is, with lines of position based on sextant observations of the sun, moon, planets and stars.

Also, there are electronic aids including radio direction finding, airborne and/or land radar, and LORAN, a long-range radio system of limited coverage. The deliberate flight into the center of a tropical storm would be undertaken only in the daytime, over the ocean, far away from land masses and under the clouds. DR navigation was required.

So, here's the bottom line. In 1950 the Navy Hurricane Hunters performed their day's work to track the location and establish the size and strength of an existing Atlantic, Caribbean or Gulf storm typically as follows: Proceed to the area of interest so as to establish en route a departure navigation fix by visual or radar contact with a geographic feature. Then, as precisely as possible, the DR track is plotted using legs of a length usually set by the interval between changes of heading. Altitude is kept low, below the base of the clouds. You have to be able to see the surface. Wind direction and force are recorded by seaman's eye; other elements of the wind triangle including air speed and heading are measured. A drift meter is also used.

The radar in the PB4Y-2 is of little value because the range is limited and the resolution poor. If there is a significant tropical storm out there, you can see signs of it, such as towering cumulus, bands of showers and thunderstorms, or variations in the air pressure and surface wind.

When the surface wind increased to 30 knots or more, we turned to place the direction from which it blows just on or ahead of the port beam. If, indeed, we were flying towards a big cyclonic circulation, the plane would be drifting to the right so much that the wind direction would fall behind the left wing. The crew commences a pattern of turning left to keep the wind ahead of the port wing. Then, with two navigators working together, an accurate plot was maintained by keeping the legs at two minutes or more.

The rain becomes torrential and continuous. The engines on the PB4Y-2 are sensitive to heavy rain because the cylinder head temperatures drop and the engines run rough. That is scary. The cowl flaps are closed, which helps, but we still worry. As the visibility drops, we have to ease down closer to the surface. It is essential the pilot and copilot keep the surface in sight. And someone must be able to read the wind direction and velocity. While I was the Meteorology Officer in the Hurricane Hunter squadron in the mid-1950s, I helped to improve the set of aerial photos of the sea surface that we used to train the flight crews in reading the wind speeds. (Selections from the set are included in the illustrations.)

Another scary thing is that the drop in atmospheric pressure makes our barometric altimeters think we are higher than we really are. The planes are equipped with an absolute altimeter, actually a ground clearance radar. The indicator, "the green worm," is back on the flight deck where one of the crew is continuously watching it and announcing the altitude above the ocean. At least one, usually the pilot's, altimeter is adjusted to match. The readout on it is then the air pressure in inches of mercury.

This is the infamous "low-level penetration" of the hurricane. Typically, the heading being flown has come around to the left at least 90 degrees. The breakthrough into the eye is dramatic: bright light, no rain and no turbulence. In the eye, the pilot stays low to get good pressure readings, then climbs to have a look at the eye wall and complete the navigation plot, check it twice and get a message back to Miami.

Winds of hurricane force (near or more than 75 knots) over the ocean tear the tops off the mountainous seas. This phenomenon has often been described by observers aboard ship. It was called *spindrift*. Seen from aircraft making a low-level hurricane penetration, the darker appearance of the water surface disappears beneath a thickening shroud of streaming torrents of spray. The tops of the seas become long streamers or curtains of fast-moving airborne ocean. Air crews have commented on the taste of sea water that finds its way into the cockpit and cabin of the old Privateers. Having already tasted the torrential rain, when they get into the rough stuff near the eye of the storm, they notice the taste is that of the ocean. Navy Hurricane Hunters from that era have described the experience as, "flying through the top layer of the ocean." The squadron ground crews were also true believers because they had found cakes and handfuls of solid salt in the crevasses of the planes' flaps and landing gear.

Let me add some thoughts about turbulence. Hurricane flying involves two types: convective turbulence occurs when you are in rain showers or thunderstorms but not flying close to the surface; mechanical turbulence is what you have during the storm penetration when you are right near the surface. The mechanical turbulence then is caused by the strong wind flowing over a very rough surface. The seas can be huge. The aircraft with all things in it is moving rapidly up and down in short but very rapid strokes. Imagine being in a vehicle going too fast over a washboard road, or maybe over closely spaced speed bumps. Whereas the convective turbulence would throw you out of your seat, the low-level turbulence makes it very difficult to write anything, or, for the navigators, to plot things on the chart.

The work of the pilot is to stay low to be out of the convective up-and-down drafts and to keep the surface in sight. He also keeps the wings nearly level. The almost continuous turning to the left must be accomplished mostly with the rudder, with very little banking. I remember how the unbalanced turns sent untethered pencils bouncing along off the right side of the navigator's table. The copilot and crew chief are constantly monitoring the engine instruments. Barring an emergency, use of the intercom is limited to terse announcements of absolute altitude (readings of vertical clearance above the ocean) and the heading.

Our second year in Miami, 1951, was a good year for me, with a long deployment to the Mediterranean and places in Europe. Maybe it was not so good for Katie, Becky and Tom. They were stuck in the cinderblock house in Opa Locka, the Navy housing area we called "Dogpatch." At least all our neighbors were squadron officers and the rent was only forty-five dollars a month. There was a lot of visiting back and forth, and we had lots of parties. One warm evening when, without any A/C all the windows in the neighborhood were open, Katie and I must have raised our voices in contentious excitement. Somebody yelled, "The Fowlers are having a fight!" So, bringing a bottle, they all gathered at our house and the party was on.

Early in March, all twelve planes of VP-23 flew to Port Lyautey in French Morocco, where the French operated a naval air station. The living conditions were not good. All the junior officers lived in a very crowded room with three-high bunks and inadequate plumbing. There was lots of flying, though. I was qualified as a first pilot and part of a crew that always flew the same plane. My log book shows that for a week in early April we operated out of the British airfield in Malta. Then on the 25th we flew to Tunisia, the 26th to Cyprus, the 28th to Ankara, Turkey, the 29th to Brindisi, and the 30th to Treviso, both in Italy. On May 1 we flew to Nice, France, and the next day, back to Port Lyautey.

While VP-23 was deployed to Port Lyautey, a Navy message called an ALNAV from Washington was circulated to all ships and stations. It contained the names of all ensigns who were promoted to Lt (JG) effective immediately. My name and that of three others in the squadron were on it. We got together, agreed on a plan and went to find the French officer in charge of the Officers Club. Our question was, "How much champagne do you have?" He said, "About fifty cases." We said, "Put it on ice." I am sure it was a wonderful wetting down party, but, for some of us, not memorable.

As I recall, each crew was assigned to a seven-day period in which to do an orientation tour of the Mediterranean area. None of us junior officers, nor, I'm sure, the enlisted crew, had any money to do serious sightseeing. But at each stop we hoofed it around as much as possible.

By the time we landed at Brindisi, a small city on the heel of Italy, we were not only broke, but out of clean underwear. Four of us joined forces and went to town. World War II was still a very fresh memory and the people loved Americans. Some youths spoke to us—offered to change some dollars to local money. We made the change with a few dollars and proceeded to a local pub. The people there laughed because what we had was Mussolini money. We described what happened and said that one of the culprits was missing one arm. We felt like dummies for having been cheated, but went on and wound up back at the Italian air base. In the wee hours, a group of local officials woke us up. They wanted us to come down to the police station. We got dressed and went with them. There was voluminous chatter but none of it in English. We were led into a dark room and the curtain in front of a window was pulled. There was a lineup. The kid with one arm was in the lineup. We were taken out to a lobby area where a brief ceremony was conducted. The precise number of U.S. dollars was presented and returned to us, followed by lots of applause and hugs all around. We expressed our gratitude and they took us back to our quarters.

On 12 May 1951, all the VP-23 aircraft departed Port Lyautey to return to Miami in three legs: to the Azores only for refueling, then to Argentia, Newfoundland, for overnight and then the long leg south to Miami. The crew I was with for the transit had an engine problem on landing at Argentia. They decided to do an engine change overnight.

I watched part of the procedure in the hangar. The guys worked hard and knew their stuff. In the morning the new engine was in place and operating, but it failed to produce full power. Something wasn't right. All eleven of the other planes were taking off. The plane commander, a Lieutenant Commander Baker, had a plan. We loaded up, taxied out, lined up and took off with three engines at takeoff power and the other idling! When out of sight of the field, Baker feathered it and we proceeded on three engines down the direct ocean route towards Florida. It was a rare learning experience of long-range ocean operation on just three engines.

We arrived at our home base, Masters Field, not long after the others. The skipper, Commander Tamny, had a welcome home ceremony planned. All the families were out there in their "bye-bye" outfits. While I was gone Katie had learned how to drive, got her license and had driven to the hangar. As soon as I had my gear and was clear of the aircraft I found her, Becky and Tom. There were hugs and kisses, then we broke for the car and went home to our cinderblock house.

At the end of January 1952, Susan had been born and the skipper had occasion to ask Katie and me how come we were producing the first squadron newborn following the deployment. Katie said, "We didn't stay at the hangar to hear the Captain's speech!" I loved her so much and was very proud of her at that moment, and also for getting her driver's license.

Susan was born in the civilian hospital at Coral Gables, Florida, on January 28, 1952. As usual, I wasn't there. I had flown up to Elizabeth City, North Carolina. There were exercises under way to demonstrate how airships ("poopy bags") could be used in coordination with patrol planes in antisubmarine warfare. I was brought back to Miami, but a day late. Unlike the first two, Katie was all by herself during this third delivery. She was fully prepared and had known all along that she would be fine in unfamiliar surroundings, but that confidence was based on my being there at her side.

Tommy had a cold on the day when Katie knew she had to go have the baby and since I wasn't there, Ernie Frederick, our neighbor, was to drive her to the hospital. Katie had comforted Tom, three and a half, and explained that she must go. She said later that if Tom had cried she would have refused to leave. He toughed it out, didn't cry, she went and the delivery was normal. Katie and Susan were perfect in every way. I should have been there.

On 18 February 1952, I reached a milestone in my training. I reached qualification as Patrol Plane Commander in the P4Y-2 (the *B* had been dropped). I also had a standard instrument rating. I still flew with the skipper's crew and when he wasn't on board I would now sign for the airplane and take the pilot's seat.

During the winter in south Florida there often was overnight and early morning fog. That February the squadron participated with other Navy units in a fleet exercise that required round-the-clock patrols. My (the skipper's) crew had completed a couple of these patrols and our next one was scheduled for takeoff in the wee hours of the night. As we readied the plane for departure the ground fog had become very heavy with almost no visibility. The tower was shut down for the night, and although the runway and taxiway lights had been left on, they could not be seen in the fog. I had no intention of being the first crew to abort and interrupt the sequence of our squadron's assigned patrols.

The Privateer had excellent, very bright landing lights controlled from the right side of the cockpit to fold down from the bottom of both wings and aim straight forward or at any downward angle. We taxied out with the copilot using the landing lights to keep us on the taxiway by seeing its edge on his side. Being very familiar with the field we arrived at the end of the long runway. I maneuvered the plane to a position exactly on the heading we knew to be that of the runway, but slightly left of center so that the centerline was illuminated by the right side landing light and clear for the copilot to see.

Chief Crissey monitored the engines to be sure they were exactly symmetrical as they came up to takeoff power. I concentrated on the instruments, released the brakes and we rolled. The copilot yelled for me to ease a little to the left. With that slight correction he indicated that we were fixed on the centerline until we lifted off and it dropped out of sight. We broke out of the top of the fog at about 700 feet.

Then at the end of the month there was an unexpected sudden change of squadrons. VP-23 was to be moved and home-ported at the Brunswick Naval Air Station near Portland, Maine. However, six aircraft and six air crews, together with half the squadron's maintenance and support personnel, were to be split off and moved to Naval Air Station Jacksonville. This was to become Weather Squadron Two (VJ-2).

The planes and crews selected were to be prepared for the hurricane reconnaissance mission of 1952. I was one of the six plane commanders. Our separation from VP-23 was to be on 11 March. There was no Navy family housing to be available in Jacksonville anytime soon, so the families were faced with a lot of things that had to be done.

I told Katie I would go up to Jacksonville and find a furnished house to rent and she should go ahead and sell our furniture. I found a nice house on Appleton Street that was available, but *not* furnished. I got Katie on the phone; she had already sold our stuff. She managed to get a crib and a bed back, and we completed the move.

Looking back on our Navy career, that was just one of fifteen moves that we made. My wonderful wife was an absolute magician. With her talent, ability and imagination, she created a home, *our* home, out of whatever shelter and furnishings were available. By this time, she had started to collect particular treasured items that for many years would define our home no matter what or where the house was. These were coveted things that helped us feel comfortable at home in that 1952 Jacksonville house and are still doing the same thing, sixty-plus years later.

My tour in Weather Squadron Two lasted only until December 1952. While I had been promoted to Lt (JG), I was still one of the very junior officers, but I was one of the most experienced hurricane pilots, after two seasons.

There was a new commanding officer of the Navy Hurricane Center, still in Miami. He wanted to make an orientation and goodwill tour of the Gulf, especially to cities in Mexico. I was given the assignment and we planned a trip to Houston, Corpus Christi, Vera Cruz, Mérida, Key West, Miami and back home. There were five passengers and their luggage. We planned enough fuel to take us to Corpus Christi, so the P4Y-2 was moderately heavy. As we taxied out, the tower said they were closing the long east-west runway and we must use the shorter northwest runway for takeoff.

The wind was OK, so I agreed, moved up to the very end of the runway and did a tight 180 to line up with as much runway as possible. In later years flying P-2 aircraft you could back up using reverse pitch, but not in the P4Y-2. We ran up the engines with the brakes locked. The checklist was complete. I looked at the tall pine trees off the far end of the runway and told my copilot to be prepared if I called for one-quarter flaps. He said OK. We set takeoff power; the crew chief confirmed everything was working. I released the brakes.

We rolled and rolled, the airspeed crawled up. We rolled some more. Most of the runway was behind us; I eased the yoke back, the nose wheel started to come off, and I shouted, "One-quarter flaps!" The extra lift kicked in and we cleared the trees. That was a learning experience with heavier loads on short runways that I never forgot.

The Atlantic hurricane season of 1952 was forgettable because there were no significant storms that posed a serious threat to the United States. The Navy Hurricane Hunters of VJ-2 stayed busy, however, flying into those that stayed in the Caribbean and out in the Atlantic. With my regular crew, including Lieutenant Bill Dean and Lieutenant (JG)s Campbell and Hemming plus Chief Crissey, in our assigned P4Y-2 I flew out of Bermuda, Trinidad and Panama as well as Puerto Rico. I logged a total of 436 hours that year and had accumulated a total of 1,500 pilot hours.

It was on 19 and 20 July that I had flown a boondoggle to New Orleans, and St. Louis, with a brief stop at Waterloo. My parents and some of Katie's family were there at the airport. Bob was getting married that very day, at Earlville, about sixty miles east of Waterloo. My mother had Bob's dress shoes that he had forgotten. They were tied up in a paper bundle. We took the shoes with us, took off in our P4Y-2, followed U.S. Highway 20 east, found the farm, made a low pass and threw out the shoes.

The other thing I remember about our brief year in that house on Appleton Street is that Bob and his new bride, Janice, came down to visit us on their honeymoon trip at the end of July 1952. We put a mattress on the living room floor. I remember when Tommy asked his mom, "Who is that girl in the bathroom with Uncle Bob?"

On 10 December 1952, my first sea duty tour came to an end. I had requested Navy Postgraduate School for my shore duty tour. I was lucky again

and had orders to the school at Monterey, California. The course started in January 1953 with graduation to be in June 1954.

Navy family housing was newly built in Monterey. We moved into a new three-bedroom home in La Mesa Village. Most of our classmates and their families were neighbors there.

The Navy was teaching meteorology in courses of 12, 18 or 24 months. The Navy called it Aerological Engineering, leading to a master's degree in 24 months or, as in my case, to a bachelor's degree in 18 months. There were about forty of us in that group.

My log book reflects that I flew at least four hours each month in 1953 and through June 1954. They call that proficiency flying. The Navy operated a small air station at Monterey for the sole purpose of keeping all the pilots who were studying there proficient. I usually flew the twin engine Beechcraft, called the "bugsmasher." But once, on May 15, 1953, I flew the PBY-5A, the amphibious version of the Catalina seaplane of "Black Cat" WWII fame.

I must digress here to share with you, dear readers, a matter that had been very much on my mind. The U.S. government had lured me into accepting a Regular Navy Commission if I would become a Naval Aviator. But, now, after five years of flight training and a first squadron tour, it hit me! What I really am is a regular U.S. Naval Officer, a Line Officer required and expected to compete with my contemporaries in all the fields of ship operations, naval warfare, history, tradition and especially leadership. As a Line Officer I wore a star above the stripes on my uniform sleeve. Officers of the Supply, Medical, Dental, Civil Engineers or Chaplains Corps were not line officers and wore their own corps symbols.

I had to be more than an aviator. I could feel it in the surroundings, and among my classmates and others I met at the P.G. school. The field in which I was competing was right there in those classrooms and not out at the airfield where we were spending at least four hours each month, as if it were recreational. I realized that promotion to O-2 (Lt (JG)) and even to 0-3 (Lt) were virtually automatic. Beyond that, the selection boards would be looking for at least competitive, if not exceptional, demonstrations of leadership, skills, abilities and potential. Knowing that I was way behind, I was desperate to figure out ways to catch up.

Sixteen years later, in 1969, I was promoted to O-6, Captain. If asked at that time how I managed to do that, the answers would have been clear, as they are now. First, Katie was my constant partner, strategist, critic and cheerleader. She made sure I did my best and never quit. Katie was also the tactical planner, counted on to know what was best and to find the way forward in decision making. Our teamwork became to be known playfully, but accurately, as, "She is in plans and I am operations." Second, the Navy offered correspondence courses to officers like me who needed to learn at least some of the naval science subjects including those taught at the U.S. Naval Academy and at NROTC. Beginning with a course on Navy Regulations and Customs in October 1949 and ending with The Gunnery Officer in 1958, I methodically tackled and actually completed twenty-five of those correspondence courses with an average grade of 3.81. And third, with Katie's encouragement, for my second shore duty tour I passed up an offer to be an admiral's aide at the North Atlantic Treaty Organization (NATO) Headquarters in Brussels in order to get a tour of duty as an NROTC instructor. More on that later.

Back to the meteorology course at Monterey. I fell in with three other guys who were just as motivated as I: Bill Ballestri, Harry Wagner and Dick Herman. We got together at least one evening each week for group study. All of the houses at La Mesa Village had dining room tables that suited our purpose. For each class, or subject that we all shared, one of us would be the study leader. The leader would concentrate on the instructor and on the material as being taught. For every test, especially the final, the leader worked up a study guide or digest of the essentials to be reviewed and, if needed, memorized. At each of our meetings the material was then beaten into the other three.

During the winter-spring of 1954, all the theory of weather observation, analysis and forecasting was gathered into a final course called Dynamic Meteorology taught by a rather grim, no-nonsense scientist. He didn't use a particular textbook. He talked a lot about the distribution and flow of energy in the atmosphere as depicted in the meanderings of the jet stream and used words like *entropy, vorticity* and *curvature.*

I was the study leader for that final course. I really worked at absorbing exactly what the man thought and what he was trying to teach us. I prepared a thorough study guide. Our instructor had emphasized the techniques used in forecasting the future location and shape of the jet stream that goes around the earth at thirty to forty thousand feet in a pattern of ridges and troughs. There was an entire catalogue of terminology and rules that he presented.

I knew there had to be a way to deal with that on the final exam. The variables were in pairs: positive-negative, accelerate-decelerate and trough-ridge. I predicted that several questions—they were to be true/false, multiple choice, fill-ins and essay—could be correctly answered if a person remembered the basic version of a rule: *positive curvature decelerates a trough.* So, I created and we all used the mnemonic device "Pacific Coast Devirgining Team" and got all those questions right. It was a three-hour exam with 120 questions. Two of our group were graded almost perfect. I had one true/false question wrong. Our study group was successful. At graduation time I was tied with another student for top academic standing.

I had orders to return for sea duty with my old squadron, the East Coast Hurricane Hunters. It was now called VW-4 and the old P4Y-2s were gone, replaced by the new Lockheed P2V Neptunes. I reported for duty according to my log book on June 23, 1954. Some of my old shipmates were still there. One young man who had been a rookie in 1952 seemed to think I had been rough on him when I had been his instructor, in the P4Y-2. Now the roles were reversed. We were in one of the early P2V-3 airplanes and I was the trainee. He was all business and was very demanding as we made many takeoff and landing exercises. He introduced emergency situations, both actual and simulated. It was hard work and he hadn't caught me in any mistakes or unprepared. He may have been disappointed or maybe he was still disgruntled about how I had been tough on him two years before.

In any event, on the next takeoff he waited until the most crucial moment, when the main gear was just breaking contact with the runway, and he chopped the starboard engine by yanking the throttle all the way back to idle. There was no simulation about it. This was a real-life emergency; a second too late to abort. I automatically applied rapid muscle power and reflex reactions maintaining control and we survived.

That young man was Joe Pausner. We've been good friends ever since. He did a good job. A less aggressive instructor pilot might have pulled that throttle back about halfway, or pulled it two seconds earlier, where an aborted takeoff on a fairly long runway would have been a good reaction, or two seconds later, when a slight reduction in power on the good engine would make the aircraft more easily controlled.

I served in VW-4 for three years. We moved into a rental house on Appleton Street, a block from the one we occupied in 1952, with Becky, Tom and Susan (ages eight, six and two). We invested in card tables, red-and-white-checked tablecloths and beer mugs. We threw darn good squadron parties. Our homemade pizza was a hit. I would get a keg and put it in a washtub full of ice. It would usually last a few days after the party. To deal with that, I would bring Roger Farrell, Pete Wendler, Bill Marsh and Frank Carney home from work with me.

I will now try to pick out a few highlights from my memory of those years, some of the best years of my life. Katie and I were madly in love. The flying was good, too.

VW-4 would have a two- or three-plane detachment stationed in San Juan during the June to October season. There was a small naval base there with an admiral and his headquarters for the Tenth Naval District. Adjacent was the Isla Grande runway and commercial air terminal, right in the city.

One of the junior officers in the squadron was Bud Fruehauf. Many of you older folks may recognize that name from seeing it on all the big eighteen-wheeler trailers on the highway. One time when my crew was in San Juan, Bud announced that his parents were to be at the Caribe Hilton for a vacation. The squadron detachment officers were invited over to their suite for a party. We all did the s-h-to-the-fifth-power—shit, shave, shower, shine and shampoo—arranged for one of our chief petty officers to stand watch and reported en masse at the Hilton. The Fruehauf "suite" was the entire penthouse floor! What a party. Somebody played the grand piano. Bud's mom called everybody to attention and explained the reason we were there was that in their stable of thoroughbred race horses a dozen or so were turning two years old and had to be named. A grand time was had by all, and I have no idea how the naming of the horses turned out.

There is another story about the San Juan Detachment that must be told. It actually happened in '51 or '52 when we were flying the P4Y-2. The historic El Moro Castle was all part of the Army's Fort Brook property. The recreation department operated a golf course on Fort Brook. The par-fives ran both ways on the big parade ground. Some of the short holes were actually laid out in the moats. The perfect tee shot would carom off the wall of the moat to make the dogleg. One day three of us were out on the par-five looking for some shade and a cold drink. We saw the Class Six Store on the adjoining street. We were reviving with a cold Coke and noticed a beverage distributor was in urgent conversation with the store manager. What we were overhearing was that it had to do with thirteen dollars per case Canadian Schenley whiskey.

One of us interjected that he might want a case of that. The manager chuckled and said, "Forget it. We're dealing with hundred case lots." We said, "Oh," and started back to the golf course. Out on the sidewalk, the wheels were churning. We looked at each other and almost in unison said, "We can do that."

And we did, too. The customs people at Isla Grande knew us and always cleared us for "reasonable and proper" amounts of untaxed booze going back to Miami. With all four of us writing checks we managed the thirteen hundred dollars. Two Army 6 x 6 trucks moved the cargo down to the flight line. We sent a personal message to the squadron XO, Commander Lou Delatour, saying we needed another aircraft down at San Juan. The squadron sent another plane. When the operation was completed, every officer and chief petty officer in the squadron got a case of Canadian Schenley for thirteen dollars.

When Lieutenant Roger Farrell and I were together in Old San Juan we liked to fly over to St. Thomas and practice precision touchdowns and short roll-outs. The runway at St. Thomas was eastward into the prevailing wind with the approach over water, but there were mountains just off the east end. It was no place for big heavy airplanes. Lightly loaded, our P2V-5J was perfectly OK there. There were no taxiways. The only turnoff was about fifteen hundred feet from the west end. We discovered that, taking turns, either one of us could make just the right approach, touch down exactly on the end of the runway, get the nose wheel down and engage both engines in reverse thrust to make that turnoff.

That may strike you as foolishness or, heaven forbid, careless irresponsibility. But both of us saw it as a demonstration of perfect coordination by man and machine. To me, it was just another example of your airplane being an extension of your body and if you knew it well enough you could control it in any situation. You knew the machine would react just the way your head, hands and feet were directing it.

With the facilities and ground support team there at the San Juan Isla Grande airport, our detachment flew local training flights regularly. Some of those training flights were used for the flight crews to become familiar with the other airfields in the Eastern Caribbean. And, that is how it happened that I visited Port au Prince, Haiti.

There was a former U.S. naval aviator who had settled in Port au Prince. He lived in a house right in the city; the backyard was at least two or three acres, all shaded by huge sprawling tropical trees. He had established a thriving business of creating and selling products made from supplies of Haitian mahogany. The main product crafted there was a nice set of salad bowls including the fork and spoon with an attractive pattern of hand-rubbed light and dark finishes. It was fascinating to watch the local people happily singing while they worked there in that yard. The big surprise, to me, was that there was no normal electric power. Men were seated on bicycle frames with the sprockets belted to drive lathe-like fixtures holding the wood as it was shaped by hand-held chisels. All of the woodworking was being done by manual labor.

I was told that the rubbing by hand started with dry steel wool and was finished with a combination of linseed oil and alcohol. The end result was beautiful and lasting. By taking advantage of several subsequent trips I managed to buy and carry home many of the larger sets of salad bowls. There was also one very large serving bowl that is still stored at my Fairfax home where Katie had it on a closet shelf. There is, also on that shelf, a mahogany lazy Susan that was manufactured by hand there in the shade behind the house in Port au Prince. Before I was finished with the Haiti mahogany, I was able to buy two coffee tables and carry them back, packed in the bomb bay of the Neptune, to our home in Jacksonville. Today one of them is happily at home with Jan and Ken in the sunroom of their wonderful home in North Carolina. During a recent visit, Susan carried the other one back with her to her home in Massachusetts.

Hurricane Hazel in 1954 is remembered for its classic size, life cycle and track. VW-4 planes were poking around it and in it two or three times a day for ten days prior to its landfall on the Carolina Coast. On the day of its discovery, a plane had flown east from Trinidad to look at a tropical disturbance or a "wave in the easterlies." The crew found the crucial evidence of a closed circulation: a slight westerly wind on its south side. Another plane was out there early the next day, and then an afternoon flight, night radar tracking and so on.

The plot of center locations showed slow steady movement due west. It reached hurricane strength and passed over the Windward Islands. The squadron was fully engaged, mostly out of San Juan. As the Public Information Officer (PIO), I was trying to generate interest among the magazine writers, newspapers and TV broadcasters. The creator of the Buzz Sawyer comic strip got interested. And a writer for *Colliers* magazine paid a visit.

Eventually the magazine article was published. It included our chart showing the size and center point of the eye for each report we had generated, and the entire life of Hazel from out on the Atlantic through the Eastern Caribbean, making a hard right turn northward through the Windward Passage between Hispaniola and Cuba, brushing by the Bahamas and up the East Coast. Landfall was at Myrtle Beach, South Carolina, on 15 October 1954.

Looking back, I can see that Hurricane Hazel was a good, perhaps the best, example of how the work of the Navy Hurricane Hunters, in those days before satellites, was the critical resource in the creation of timely and accurate warnings. Property was, of course, destroyed, but people were warned and able to safely evacuate.

Subsequently a hurricane named Connie threatened the East Coast in August 1955. Roger and I with his well-trained crew flew the storm out in the Atlantic on the 8th. The projected path stirred up some interest by the New York City news media, including the recently born TV networks. A few phone calls raised a nibble from NBC. *The Today Show* with Dave Garroway, live and in black and white, was brand new. As PIO, I engineered a deal with NBC. The squadron CO readily approved. Roger, the crew and I would track Connie by radar overnight on the 10th, land at Floyd Bennett Field out on Long Island at a time calculated so we would taxi to a stop, disembark and face the NBC cameras right at seven a.m. We did exactly that, and we appeared on *Today* shortly after seven o'clock. Dave stayed in the studio; another guy did a quick interview. *The Today Show* crew asked us to stay put and be ready to re-enact the whole thing for the eight o'clock *Today* segment. They chatted with all the crew and asked me to help them dig up some better human interest material.

At this point, I must introduce Ensign John Anderson. He had just reported for duty with VW-4 having finished the one-year course in

Aerological Engineering. He was assigned to our crew for this mission. He knew nothing about the P2V-5JF. He was strapped down in our Neptune facing aft, behind the wing. In that position, he experienced his very first takeoff. It was loaded with fuel for a long flight, and for him it must have been horrendous. The two R-3350 engines were at full power and the two jet engines were also screaming at full power. When the brakes were released the acceleration squeezed the breath out of him.

Back at Floyd Bennett, I nominated Anderson for the human interest interview. The eight o'clock routine was performed. The announcer asked John about being new in the squadron. John confirmed that, indeed, this hurricane flight was his first time in the airplane. The next question was: "Were you scared?"

Answer: "Scared? I was frightened out of my wits."

Question: "What was it about flying in Connie that scared you the most?"

Answer: "The takeoff."

Our whole crew spent that night at NBC's expense in a Manhattan hotel. What's more, they had me promise to fly back to New York City a few days later to be a contestant on *What's My Line*. I did that. I can remember that John Charles Daly was the moderator and the panel was made up of Bennett Cerf, Dorothy Kilgallen, Fred Allen and Arlene Francis. I was to be in civilian clothes saying I was from Waterloo, Iowa. My line was *Navy Hurricane Hunter*. They didn't guess it, and NBC later sent me a check for fifty dollars. Now I wish—oh how I wish—I had saved that *What's My Line* check.

There is one more memorable experience of deliberate skill, teamwork and intrepidity that will wrap up what I have to share with you about hurricane hunting in the 1950s, and that is the story of Hurricane Janet in 1955.

In my second tour of duty with VW-4, I was the Meteorology Officer and PIO. Commander Dale Allen was the CO. Commander Nick Brango was the XO. We were flying the P2V-5JF with the two jet engines hanging from the wings outboard of the R-3350s. I was a qualified plane commander, but I usually flew with Roger Farrell's crew and shared the first pilot time with him. It was an excellent crew with lots of experience in hurricanes.

Lieutenant (JG) Jim Morris was the third pilot. He was the guy in the right seat on that flight into Janet. When we broke out of the heavy stuff into the eye everybody relaxed a little. Jim released his shoulder harness, leaned over to pick up a dropped pencil and punched out the starboard engine with his parachute harness D-ring. That was a real shock in that particular location to see one of the props at parade rest.

The storm was big, getting bigger and meandering westward south of Jamaica. Janet had been tracked by crews flying out of San Juan. Our crew and one other were being sent down to Guantánamo from Jacksonville to pick up the coverage. The other crew was Lieutenant Commander Grover Windham, with Lieutenant Tom Greany in the right seat. Farrell and I flew out to the vicinity of the hurricane for night tracking by radar on 25 September. The storm was huge, centered south and slightly east of Jamaica on a westerly course. We landed at GTMO at about three a.m. At daybreak I briefed Windham and his crew for their low-level penetration flight on 26 September. They had two news reporters from Canada going with them to get a firsthand story of how it is done. That was the tragic flight that never returned. Just about the time they should have been penetrating the hurricane their radio transmission stopped. The aircraft with all on board disappeared and nothing was ever found. All of us at Guantánamo and the VW-4 people at Jacksonville were shocked and grief-stricken. Katie and Roger's wife, Gloria, were among those offering comfort and attending to the wives and families of the missing crew.

It was most likely that Janet would be turning to a more northerly track, and it was crucial to know if, when and where that was happening. Roger Farrell, with me and the rest of his crew, with instructions from Miami, were preparing to fly into Janet early on the 27th of September. We departed and flew over the area, south of Jamaica, where the loss of the other plane occurred. We knew there was very little chance of seeing anything. The APS-20 radar in the P-2 was very good for showing precipitation returns out to a hundred miles. We had a clear depiction of the north half of the storm. We proceeded westward around it and farther west toward the Yucatán Channel and the west end of Cuba.

Out there in the Western Caribbean is Swan Island, where a few U.S. Weather Bureau and Geological Survey men were located. There was little else on the island except lots of tall palm trees and a few grazing cattle. Janet was a very powerful storm. The latest warnings, as confirmed by what we were seeing so far, had the eye of the hurricane passing directly over Swan Island later that day. We made a low pass and spoke to the men by radio. They had already been warned. They would all take refuge in the thick concrete seismic vault. That vault contained the seismographic instruments that sensed and recorded the trembling of the earth as part of a worldwide network. There were wishes of good luck all around and the P-2 was turned back toward Janet.

I was at my position in the Plexiglas enclosure in the bow of the plane. There were air pressure, outside temperature, air speed and heading instruments plus the pressure and green worm altitude indicators. I was on the intercom and was responsible for wind force estimates, absolute altitude and the ordering of heading changes.

We had used the radar to look for an avenue between spiral bands or any other indication of an easier place to enter the storm. There were no such things. On radar, the near side of Janet presented an extremely dense semicircle of precipitation echo. It is my interpretation, having experienced a number of low-level penetrations and having studied the APS-20 radar return of many tropical storms, that when an intense storm has extremely low pressure in the center, the pressure gradients near the center are so steep that the winds would be well over 100 to 150 knots. Then the radar beam is seeing the airborne top layer of the ocean mixed with the heavy rain. Moreover, when you see it from the bow station of the P-2 you are shocked to see the wind-driven seas, having built up to mountainous height, are being flattened out because the tops are being blown away by the extreme winds.

These were among the memories I still have of that day, as we completed a spiraling track into the eye of Janet. I knew that Roger was straining, successfully, to keep the wings level, to maintain a scant few hundred feet above the water and to keep skidding around to the left. He was also successful in avoiding the disaster of being sucked up into the maelstrom and losing sight of the surface. I could see that we were flying in salt water and that the pressure was falling rapidly. There was no way out except to break inside the eye wall. That's what we did!

Roger Farrell and his wife, Gloria, came to visit me recently. We talked about our flight into Janet. Here are his memories of it in his own words:

> Barometric pressure was 982 mb when we started the penetration. When we got in the eye the pressure was 928 mb. The diameter of the eye was less than 20 miles. It was a

very tight storm with very high circulation velocity. During the penetration a ball-peen hammer rose up in front of me on my left side and crossed in front of my eyes, and then back across my right shoulder. Then as the aircraft was moved by the violent storm the ball-peen hammer crashed into the sub bay of the aircraft, and was never found.

Our barometer and altimeters indicated the lowest pressure near the surface inside the eye to be 928 millibars. We looked in awe at the inside of a perfectly round eye wall structure. The aircraft and all hands in it were checked out and found to be in good shape. The radio reports were sent. We climbed up in a spiral to over 15,000 feet. The escape from the eye of Janet was relatively easy, picking a path between, or at least through, the less severe parts of thunderstorms.

Today, fifty-nine years later, I try my best to remember how it was, what I was thinking, as we powered on through a torrent of rain mixed with cloud and windblown sea. There is no memory except that of total, intense concentration. We had obviously entered the most violent conditions we had ever seen. My job was to see the surface, read the wind direction and feed a steady stream of heading adjustments to Roger. What was also obvious was that the wind force had increased to where it nearly equaled our air speed—150 knots. We were skidding about 45 degrees to the right of our heading which was constantly being turned to the left so that the wind direction remained ahead of the left wing.

Remembering that flight into Janet, Roger spoke of his struggle to keep the wind direction ahead of the left wing while controlling the altitude to stay out of the ocean, yet able to see it. He remembers that the break into the eye was incredibly sudden. He knew he must keep us low, close to the surface in order to measure the minimum surface pressure. The pressure altimeters in the cockpit are precise barometers. When the pilot adjusts the pressure setting for the needle to show our absolute altitude, the setting would read the existing air pressure. We circled low in the eye of Janet. He noted many readings, the lowest of which was 928 millibars. My barometer in the bow station agreed. With that done, the navigators and radioman were preparing and sending our report to Miami.

Roger remembers that we established a spiraling climb inside the eye. The radar operator, Chief Petty Officer Willy O'Neal, kept a close eye on the depiction on radar of the maelstrom that swirled around us. The relief and relaxation that all of us in the crew were experiencing was interrupted by the episode of Jim Morris's parachute harness D-ring feathering the prop and stopping the starboard engine. With a minimum of cursing, Roger unfeathered it and got the power back on. The climbing spiral, with the appearance of being inside a barrel, continued.

There was no comment about it, but I suspect I wasn't the only one to think about our squadron mates who, just twenty-four hours previously, had disappeared. I thought about the grieving families, the two news reporters from Canada and the two regular members of that crew who stayed behind to make room.

Roger also remembers how we climbed to a pressure altitude of 15,000 feet. Using the radar, we selected the easiest way out, made our exit and eased back down to 10,000 feet before anybody noticed any breathing discomfort. The next day, 28 September 1955, we flew back to Jacksonville.

Years later I read a report published by one of the weather guys who had survived the passage of Janet at Swan Island. He wrote how the intensity of the storm had snapped off the tops of all the tall palm trees up at about the 25-foot level. At the storm's height of intensity, during the first half, the pressure dropped so rapidly that all the cattle died from the bursting of their stomachs and other internal organs. Similarly, a look around during the eye's passage revealed that the refrigerators and freezers all had exploded their doors off. Fortunately, there were no casualties among the human survivors.

1956 was a wonderful year for our family—in our second house on Appleton Street. Becky would turn ten, Tommy, eight that summer, and Susan was four in January. Roger Farrell remembers stopping by to give me a ride to work. Susan would let him in the back door and tell him she needed help getting the cereal down from the top cupboard.

Katie was pregnant and, for the first time, I was expected to be there during the final waiting days and at the hospital. Also for the first time, it would be at a Navy hospital, the U.S. Naval Hospital Jacksonville, Florida. When the time came in early October there were a couple of false alarms, and then on October 7 Katie was in the hospital but not quite ready to deliver. I was told I could not be in the delivery room; I got antsy about the kids being alone at the house, told the nurse to call me and went home. Janine Lynn was born without further delay and I was allowed to see her and Katie about an hour later. I had preserved my record of never being there for the births of our children. Jan was indeed a beautiful baby. Upon inspection by the other kids, it was Susan who said, "God must really love us. He gave us the prettiest one." Jan is still my beautiful baby.

It came to pass that in the summer of 1957 I was due for shore duty again. While Katie and I had considered the offer of an admiral's aide's assignment in Brussels, we opted instead for a tour as an NROTC instructor. My orders were to the NROTC unit at Tulane University in New Orleans.

Jan was six months old, Becky, eleven, Tom, nine, and Susan, five. We loaded up and went to Waterloo. In my usual cavalier fashion I left Katie and the kids there, took the car and drove to Northwestern University campus in Chicago for two weeks of "charm school."

Then, it was down to New Orleans. There was a newly constructed housing development in the suburb of Metairie. We bought one of the brand new three-bedroom houses and moved in. It was wonderful having both air conditioning and a dishwasher.

I had already been promoted to O-3 (Lt) and had accumulated 2,400 flight hours. My plan was to get the most out of the three-year tour with two NROTC summer shipboard cruises, and learn as much as possible about all facets of ship operations. My tail hook contemporaries serving on carriers were being exposed to some of it, but patrol plane drivers were considered by the "black shoe" Navy, especially "boat school" graduates, to have little or no selection potential for senior officer promotion. (The aviators wore green or khaki uniforms and brown shoes. Surface warfare officers had to wear black shoes.)

I was the instructor for the senior class, teaching celestial navigation, maneuvering board, bridge procedures, tactical communications and rules of the road. Learning all that was a daunting challenge. I did a lot of reading, and, for the most part, stayed one day ahead of the class. There were about twenty-five of them, a smart and dedicated group of young men.

One of the well-known names in Louisiana was then, and most likely still is, McIlhenny. You've seen it on that little bottle of Tabasco pepper sauce. I saw the name a lot while I was teaching at Tulane. One of my first-class midshipmen had that name and he was of that family. What's more, he was on the football team. As faculty, Katie and I had tickets to the home games that were played in the Tulane stadium, better known then as the Sugar Bowl. I honestly don't remember seeing my student play on the field. Mr. McIlhenny was not doing well in my class. The informal, but official, spoken word had been passed down: "Mr. McIlhenny must not fail his senior year of Naval Science." I really wanted him, along with all his classmates, to know celestial navigation and the other shipboard operations topics. He understood, spent time one on one with me, learned the stuff and he passed.

One of the Tulane alumni had donated an officer's dress sword each year that was to go to the NROTC graduate with the highest grade in Rules of the Road. My almost impossible task was to identify the winner. They all wanted that sword, and memorized all of the purely precise and objective body of material involved. We went through the motions of a lengthy test that they all aced. Then I tried some essay questions and some interview-style oral questions. With that I subjectively identified the winner and sidestepped the glares of the losers.

The staff at the NROTC unit consisted of five officers, two or three chiefs and a Marine sergeant. The Marine officer was Major Bob Barrow, who went on to be the Commandant of the Marine Corps.

At the beginning of each year during freshman orientation we would recruit new "contract" midshipmen who, upon graduation, would get a Naval Reserve commission. The "regular" midshipmen were winners of Navy scholarships and would earn USN commissions. At the start of each academic year all midshipmen were asked to cough up some cash for the party fund. I was the guy on the staff assigned to administer the fund and plan two midshipmen parties each year. The one in the spring was traditionally scheduled to be during Mardi Gras.

One year while we lived in New Orleans we were able to rent the American Legion hall on Royal Street, but only during the day. Katie helped me chaperone it. Most of the mids brought girls. We had recorded music and lots of beer. It was a great success. Each year our family went down to watch the Mardi Gras parades. And for Susan's sixth birthday we all went for lunch to the famous Antoine's French restaurant in the Quarter.

In August 1959, on my thirty-third birthday, Katie surprised me with a wonderful gift. She had spoken to a neighbor whose job was that of a teaching golf professional. She had saved her money and had arranged for that guy to select a set of clubs for me and to also give me a golf lesson. Wow! What a thrill—a gift that has gone on giving for the rest of my life. I have never thanked her enough. That first lesson was so important, possibly even more important than the first set of clubs. It meant that my early learning was done with the correct grip and a firm knowledge of the fundamentals. Over the span of fifty-some years, I have thoroughly enjoyed golf at a respectable level of skill and an established handicap—never better than 14, but always able to break 100 until about age eighty—and have picked up not one, not two, but three holes-in-one!

The very essence and definition of a wonderful life, for me, has been my sixty-nine years with Katie. The landscape of the path we travelled through love, marriage and family has, of course, had its highs and lows. Together, we were able to find a way to accentuate and sustain the highs, and to resolve or otherwise deal with the lows. The blessings in my life have been monumental. Among the greatest were those given or initiated by my wife, especially the birth of our four children; a prime example among the lesser ones was that 1959 gift of golf.

There was a naval air station on the south shore of Lake Pontchartrain. There were S-2, twin-engine Grumman ASW planes and also SNB twin-engine Bugsmashers. One of the other officers at Tulane was also an aviator. I had maintained my instrument qualification, so together we went on a lot of cross-countries. Our favorite was a two-day trip down to Laredo Air Force Base on the Rio Grande in Texas. It was about four hours each way so we overnighted in the Air Force BOQ. While there we usually walked across the bridge and checked out Nuevo Laredo on the Mexican side. An old lady had a cooking fire going in the middle of a street. She would roll out corn dough and cook the tortillas on a hot flat rock. I bought a dozen to take home. The ones we didn't eat right away were frozen to use later.

As a member of the faculty during my first year at Tulane I was required to take a basic course in computers. We learned about binary counting and the concept of microscopic switches and transistor circuits. I realized I could also undertake a master's degree, all expenses paid, curriculum. I was accepted in the mathematics department as a candidate for a master's. That was to be during the second and third year of the three-year tour. In the fall semester of 1958, I completed a course in differential equations, but then, before I was enrolled in the next one, I was told that we were to move to Newport, Rhode Island, for me to attend the Command and Staff course at the Naval War College, class of 1960. We were to move in June of 1959.

We would have to sell our lovely new house in Metairie. That part of the city was built on reclaimed swamp that was several feet below sea level. There were huge pumping stations along the shore of the lake. Canals and drainage ditches collected the rain and groundwater. It was pumped up into Lake Pontchartrain. In May 1959, a tropical storm came up from the Gulf and dumped about seven inches of rain beyond the limit that the pumps were designed to handle. The water filled up the streets, then the yards right up to the level of the slabs the houses were built on. The *For Sale* sign was sticking up out of the water, and prospective buyers could not reach our street. We had to leave the house in the hands of the real estate agent.

We found a perfect three-story, older New England-style house with a separate double garage to lease for a year in Middletown, a suburb of Newport. We were very lucky. Another officer had a change of orders making it suddenly available. Katie and I were both thirty-three years old; the kids, thirteen, eleven, seven and three. We all enjoyed a wonderful year there in Newport. Our traveling home, with all its love, character and expanding inventory of familiar furnishings, had found what was, so far, the best fit for the family. The finished bedroom with a half-bath up on the third floor was Tom's. He had to go down a steep flight of stairs to reach the bathroom he shared with his sisters.

Paul Dorweiler, Katie's great uncle, was an insurance professional working for Aetna in Hartford, Connecticut, where he lived in a gentleman's club. He was Grandma Mersch's bachelor brother, the one who had offered financial help for Katie and some of her cousins to attend college. There had been eight children in the Dorweiler family—homestead farmers in Northwest Iowa. Every one of them graduated from college. I will always remember when, with Katie, I attended one of the Dorweiler's family reunions during the war. It was impressive to see such a large extended family that grew from nineteenth century homesteaders.

Katie's handwritten letters to Uncle Paul were carefully saved and in recent years, long after his death, were returned to us. Katie was an excellent writer; she had been the feature editor of our high school paper and started her college education in English and journalism. Her letters to Uncle Paul all were done with pen and ink in her perfect penmanship. I have just now read all twenty-six of them, dated from 1941 to 1958, each with a three-cent stamp. In the letter dated June 6, 1944, and postmarked June 7, twelve-thirty p.m., Katie writes about the thrill of high school graduation and her very serious thoughts about what the future holds. The final segment is quoted as follows:

> . . . I will be prepared to earn some extra money freelance writing for newspapers. My present journalism instructor recommended either Minnesota or Iowa University for the remainder of my training.
>
> Another thing that really makes me think about things is the invasion. I didn't hear about it until I got to work this morning. (I'm selling shoes at Sears and Roebucks for the summer.) It seemed like everybody was happy about it because it was the "beginning of the end," but, yet, you could tell that they were tense inside, wondering whose boyfriend or brother wouldn't come back. All the stores in Waterloo closed for one hour so that everyone could go to church for a prayer service. I was surely glad my boyfriend was sitting beside me instead of flying a plane over Germany. (He'll go into the Air Corps when he's 18 in August.)
>
> It just doesn't seem possible that people who call themselves civilized can ever get mixed up in a war. Here's hoping it's the last time graduates have to go out into a world at war.
>
> Thank you again for the present. I'll try to invest it in something for the future.
>
> Love – your niece,
> Kathryn

It was the fall of 1959 when Uncle Paul came to stay a few days with us in Newport. When Katie spoke about the second floor bedroom he was to use, he emphatically said, "No way. I'm going to sleep on the third floor with Tommy." He did and we all still treasure the memories of his visit.

During that year at the War College, each student wrote a research paper on strategy. We were assigned two to a room for private study. Each student had a safe for keeping classified material. My roommate was Ed Waller who was also a multi-engine patrol plane pilot. It was a presidential election year, so Ed decided to do a study of the strategic implications in the comparative abilities and leadership potential of the candidates. The staff told him he couldn't do that because the active duty military in our country do not mess with politics. Ed did it anyway, and used our study room to debate and explore the virtues and faults of all the candidates. I agreed with his analysis and conclusion that Jack Kennedy was best qualified to be Commander in Chief. Ed survived the staff criticism, and I believe he later became a rear admiral.

My research paper was on climate change with the focus on the Arctic Ocean and surrounding land masses. The question concerned man's influence, both from unintended consequences of human activity, and also speculation that humans could deliberately manipulate the sensitive sea ice cover of the Arctic Ocean. I concluded that, one way or another, the sea ice of the Arctic Ocean would disappear sometime in the foreseeable future with great strategic consequences in what was then the full-blown Cold War, as open sea lanes across the Arctic would drastically change the existing isolation of the Soviet Union. Now, in the second decade of the twenty-first century, it has happened.

Chapter III
The 1960s

Weston wished we could have stayed in that Newport house, but my orders in the spring of 1960 were to proceed to Jacksonville, Florida, to be part of the Patrol Squadron community specializing in the antisubmarine warfare mission. We had heard about a new housing development called Ortega Hills right across the highway from the main gate of the Naval Air Station. We signed up to buy one of the houses that were under construction. We moved in that summer and lived in that same house on Ortega Hills Drive for seven years. When we left there in 1967 Becky was twenty-one, a junior at Florida State University in Tallahassee; Tom, nineteen, was finishing his plebe year at the Naval Academy; while Susan, fifteen, and Jan, eleven, were still at home.

During those seven years I served right there at the same set of hangars at NAS Jax: first, on Fleet Air Wing ELEVEN staff; then as the Maintenance Officer and the Operations Officer with VP-5; as the Operations Officer and the Executive Officer of VP-30; and, finally, as the Executive Officer and Commanding Officer of VP-7.

I was the Plans Officer on the staff of Commander Fleet Air Wing ELEVEN from 1960 to 1962. The Cold War, almost forgotten today, included the nuclear weapon standoff between America with her NATO allies and the Soviet Union. The standoff had reached a pinnacle of tension during the Cuban Missile Crisis that culminated in October 1962. Soviet Premier Khrushchev had started the placing of medium-range ballistic missiles with nuclear warheads in Cuba. The missiles were so big they had to be transported as deck cargo on ships. Aerial surveillance by long-range patrol aircraft was essential. That is one of the things that VP squadrons do best. The FAW-11 squadrons maintained a detachment at Key West to keep a 24/7 eye on the shipping in and out of Cuba. The resulting photography of the shipboard deck-loaded missiles en route to Cuba, along with that taken by high altitude reconnaissance jets showing the missile launch sites, were the proof of the enemy threat.

The crisis atmosphere among Americans, especially in Florida, was growing. Jan, Susan, Tom and Becky were in the same public school system but in four different schools. First-grader Jan told us about practicing "duck and cover," and, if there was an attack, or imminent threat, she would be evacuated to a town called Stark, Florida. Our other kids would similarly be evacuated, to other places, all by train. Obviously, a nuclear attack on Northeast Florida, just like a midair collision, would spoil your whole day. But it was a real stretch on our scale of fear to deal with an expedition to four remote, unfamiliar places to find the kids. We worried about that.

Nikita Khrushchev played a gut-wrenching game of chicken with President Jack Kennedy. With the photographic proof, Kennedy was able to expose the Soviet deception and to negotiate a peaceful removal of the threat. Today, in our world the way it is, there are parallel situations, especially in the Middle East, that will require our President to have the knowledge, temperament and ability to similarly protect us from disaster. I worry about that, too.

Many of the squadron deployments were to the Italian NATO airbase at Sigonella just outside the city of Catania, on the east coast of Sicily, just at the foot of Mount Etna, the 13,000-foot active volcano. Needless to say, the minimum safe altitude flying under visual rules in that area was about 15,000 feet.

We frequently landed at or staged operations out of various airfields on the islands of Malta, Sardinia and Crete. The only place in the Med area where we could give our P2Vs a thorough washing was at the Wheelus Air Base in Tripoli, Libya. My crew would fly down there early in the morning. All hands would work together at the wash rack, cleaning the salt off the plane. Then we could all go to the beach, or some of us would go to the golf course. That course at Tripoli is the only one I ever saw that had zero blades of grass anywhere on the course, including the greens. It was all flat desert, sand and a few small rocks. When arriving at the "green," you used a burlap drag to smooth out the footprints on your path to the hole.

My favorite story about a Cold War experience was set at Incerlik Air Base near Adana, Turkey. I took a three-plane detachment over there from Sigonella. Our task was to do a low-level search over part of the Black Sea. I remember the flight over the mountains of Turkey and then finding a hole through the broken layers of clouds to let down. For us it was totally uncontrolled airspace. We were to fly in electronic silence, not radiating any radar or radio transmissions. Our search was with the magnetic airborne detector designed for finding submerged subs. We didn't find anything, but a Soviet seaplane came out of its Crimea base to check on us. We finished what we were doing and got the heck out of there.

While at Incerlik we went on liberty and saw some of the city of Adana. Walking in the city we were spoken to by a man, apparently a policeman. He indicated we should proceed through a gate and down the street beyond. It turned out to be the women's prison. The women inmates were allowed to advertise there in the display windows along the street. We got out of there and inquired about the bazaar market. Finding it, I wound up buying the big round brass tray that hangs today above our fireplace. There was plenty of room in the bomb bay of the P-2 to get it all the way home.

In Sicily we were acquainted with a family that operated a marble quarry. After returning to Jax and, among other things, talking to Katie about marble, we did some measurements. It wasn't long until I deployed to Sigonella again. My friend took me to the quarry. We picked out a slab that he promised would, when cut and polished, be white with streaks of black and grey. His crew cut pieces for a coffee table, two end tables and another 40-inch round table. Before I flew back home some months later those pieces were finished, beveled, polished and packed in crates. I also hauled them back home in the bomb bay. I'm looking at them now out on the porch. Beautiful.

As noted, we flew out of the NATO airfield in Sicily, that was named Sigonella. When the squadron officers put on a musical show for the station officers and their families (Italian and American), we performed a final number that used the tune of "Nothing could be finer than to be in Carolina . . ." only our version went "Nothing could be sweller than to be in Sigoneller . . ." The last line of that song was, "If you gave an enema to this dear old globe, this is the place where you'd stick the tube . . . Nothing could be sweller than to be in Sigoneller in the mo-o-orn-ning!"

Sigonella was properly called a Naval Air Facility. In keeping with the finest traditions of the service, the folks who were stationed there worked valiantly and laboriously to create a nine-hole golf course. The only available acreage was steep, very rocky and grossly overgrown. After about a year of hard work the only acceptable areas for the purpose had been selected, cleared, leveled and sodded. They were called "greens."

I was with the next squadron to arrive there on deployment. The big news was that the Sigonella golf course was ready for play. I was one of the first volunteers. Personal golf clubs and golf balls were not allowed. Your choice from a dozen sets of used clubs were available as part of the green fee. They had a mail-order supplier of bulk quantities of used golf balls. The terrain was really rocky. Wooden tees were allowed, and needed, for all shots except on the green. The trail from tee to green was barely negotiable, but fun. The local rule was: Don't look for a lost ball. Go to the vicinity and tee up another without penalty.

Aside from marble, one of the local treasures that could be bought cheap and brought home was the olive jug. It was made of green glass and manufactured locally. It was a pear-shaped thing, about 20 inches tall and 16 inches in greatest diameter. There were two basic designs. One had a neck that narrowed to an opening of just more than an inch. It was used for olive oil. The neck of the other was almost five inches wide and it was used for olives. That is the one I bought. Like all of the others, it came wrapped in a basket-like covering made of woven sisal with two handles. On arrival at Jacksonville, the U.S. Customs and Agriculture inspector had me remove the sisal cover (I had intended to, anyway) because of the agriculture rules. That jug is proudly displayed in the antique room divider in the family room that Katie found and had me rebuild to hold our 46-inch TV.

Katie was active in the Jacksonville Officers Wives Club, and in 1962 she was elected president. The big annual charity event sponsored by the OWC was the Magnolia Ball. It was a major social event with white dress uniforms, and long formal gowns. It was held in the Officers Club building surrounded by magnolia trees on the banks of the St. Johns River. The OWC committees worked feverishly on the charity fundraising program, decorations, food, etc. The big day was to be November 22, 1963. The whole country was shocked that day when it was known that President Kennedy had been shot and had died. Katie knew immediately that the ball must be cancelled and rescheduled. The decorations committee chairperson just couldn't accept that. The work had all been done. She couldn't imagine her group doing it all again. Members involved with procuring the food were also strongly against cancellation.

Katie didn't waste any time debating. She got the NAS Commanding Officer on the phone. His decision was quick and final. The Magnolia Ball, to be held the night the President was assassinated, was cancelled. The officers' wives rallied around their club president, and, along with them, I was very proud of her leadership in the face of a tragic turn of events.

There was another unrelated tragedy along about that same time. The patrol squadron mission was training for the hunting and killing of enemy submarines. At that time the potentially hostile subs were all diesel battery powered. The subs had to snorkel or operate on the surface to recharge their batteries. Accordingly our weapons and tactics included the ability to kill a sub found on or near the surface. Such an opportunity would most likely be at night, so we were practicing attacks using wing-mounted rockets that were aimed with the help of a powerful search light.

One of the small lakes in North Central Florida was designated a military bombing range. It had a wood structure in the middle used as a target. Our night flights with firing runs on the target used real rockets, but without warheads. The practice runs were to train the searchlight operator, as well as to improve the pilot's skill in getting the target in his gunsight, and scoring hits. Each run was concluded by pulling out with safe clearance above the lake. Lieutenant Commander Walt Gardner was a very good friend. He, with five other friends and shipmates, were killed when their plane, doing night searchlight runs, crashed into that lake. His widow asked me to act as official escort for Walt's remains, traveling by train to Arlington National Cemetery. I did that and participated in the ceremony to present to her the flag that draped his casket. It was a tragic accident that should never have happened. That is all I have to say about it.

Patrol Squadron 30 at Jacksonville was the replacement training squadron for pilots and other aircrew being assigned to VP squadrons on the East Coast. During my tour with VP-5 I had been promoted to O-5, Commander. Katie and I were anticipating that I would stay there and move up to be CO of VP-5. It was not to be. Some other slightly more senior officer aced me out. Instead, I had orders to join VP-30. I started there as Operations Officer and moved up to XO. While at VP-30 I was doing a lot of emergency procedure training of experienced pilots being qualified for the first time in P-2 aircraft.

One day, Navy electrician's mate Jim Shadle, Katie's younger brother, and Jim's cousin Wally, a Marine PFC, called. They were both in Jacksonville in uniform passing through for some reason. I was about ready for my next local training flight. I told Jim and Wally to get over to the VP-30 hangar and go with me. They showed up. I gave them a quick look at the inside of the P-2, strapped them in and off we went. We used the nearby Mayport runway that day, making fifteen or twenty touch-and-go landings, takeoffs and circuits around the field on a very hot summer day. You will have to ask Uncle Jim whether or not that was fun.

There was to be a change of command at VP-30. Commander Bruce Smith was being relieved by Commander Don Gately. As XO, I was to be commander of the all-hands formation lined up by divisions and departments in full dress whites including officers' swords. Admiral Mattern, Commander Fleet Air Wings, Atlantic, would be on the platform witnessing the ceremony and delivering a speech. There was a Navy marching band, also.

There was plenty of room in the hangar; and the plan, when the ceremony was complete, was that the squadron would pass in review. The band would lead the parade, crossing in front of the spectator seating and the platform, followed by all the divisions of troops.

Keep in mind this was all quite new to me. My Academy contemporaries had done parades like this every week at Annapolis. This was a once-in-a-lifetime event for me. We sure as hell didn't do this in Antarctica. More on that later.

My instructions were to order the parade to commence as soon as the admiral's speech was finished. All hands were at parade rest as the ceremony proceeded. When it came the admiral's turn it seemed to me that everything was moving along splendidly; the public address system was working fine. After a while the tone of what he was saying sounded to me like he was wrapping it up. When he turned away from the mike and walked back toward the group on the platform, I recognized that as my signal. I snapped to, called the staff to attention, gave them an about-face and yelled, "Squadron, pass in review!" Department heads and division officers relayed the command, the band struck up a march and off we went.

An hour or so later, I was with the others at a reception at the Officers Club. It had been hinted to me that maybe I had screwed up by ordering the parade to begin a bit too soon. Some suggested that the admiral seemed a little confused and put off when he finished his handshakes with the principals and turned back to the mike to finish his remarks. I whispered a question to Commander Gately about it and asked him if I should apologize to the admiral. Gately said, "I wouldn't speak to him if I were you."

My log book in the 1960s records more than forty of my flights were in the UO-1. It was a little twin-engine, tricycle gear, low-wing, four-place utility plane built by Piper. It was very user friendly and well equipped for instrument flying.

The Air Wing staff would make official coordination visits to the Navy's Underwater Sound Monitoring Stations (SOSUS) on islands in the Bahamas and along the East Coast. I especially enjoyed going to the SOSUS station at Cape Hatteras. There was another one on the Carolina coast where a short runway was cut out of the forest of southern pines. On my first flight to that one on a hot summer day, the plane was loaded with four of us. After we finished our business with the SOSUS guys, we went back out to the Piper. I made sure that no additional fuel or any other weight had been added. From down on the ground it looked like the pine trees had grown. We had taken a good look at them during the approach and landing. On takeoff we had a much closer look.

From April 1965 through May 1967 I served in VP-7, a year as XO, and then a year as Commanding Officer. The squadron made a long seven-month deployment to the Mediterranean. I flew 784 hours in the SP-2H while in VP-7. While I had the squadron in the Med, we flew out of Souda Bay in Crete, and later out of an airfield near Cagliari in Sardinia. The idea was to practice the concept of advance base operations when a patrol squadron is supported by a ship serving as a tender. All of our food, shelter, aircraft maintenance, ground equipment and non-flight crew personnel were aboard the tender. The concept worked well, and we saw parts of these islands not usually seen by such as we. As squadron skipper, I enjoyed the use of one of the jeeps that always came off the ship first and assigned for my use.

Looking back, I must conclude that life in the head shed of one of those squadrons was mostly paperwork. I can't dredge up any more real memorable happenings, except that, during my year as skipper, the squadron air and ground operations were accident free. It was also important to me that all of our squadron people enjoyed a year of unblemished morale and welfare. I was then and will always be proud of the officers and men of VP-7.

Tom was graduating from high school in '66. Becky was already attending Florida State University and living in the dorm in Tallahassee. Tom had applied for a Navy ROTC scholarship, and had been accepted to go to the University of Wisconsin. Katie and I were very proud of him for that, but when the time came, our congressman had selected Tom as an alternate and then he was appointed to join the Naval Academy class of 1970. And, we were really proud of Tom for that.

Now, let's break away from the makeshift timeline of this adventure. I will try to shed some light on just what, and why, I am doing all this scribbling on these scratch pads. This seems to be a memoir of the path taken by my life, produced entirely from my aging memory. The only substantial reference source I've used, so far, is my Aviator's Log Book. Actually it is five log books, including one from Parks College, where it is recorded that my flying career commenced on August 1, 1946. The final entry in my Navy log book was February 22, 1974. The final entry of my pilot hours was 3.5, on 28 December 1973, in a UH-1N helicopter of VXE-6 in Antarctica. My total career pilot hours, including those from Parks, were 5,213.4! The closest thing to an accident I had ever been involved in, during all those hours, was the late wire incident on my sixth carrier landing in 1949.

So, this storytelling is drawn mostly from what I can remember. It's about how the hard work of curb-hopping and long days at the filling station evolved into layers of education which, along with a most wonderful marriage, built the foundation for a successful career and family life sequence. I am a survivor, abundantly blessed by God, and more often than not, with Good Luck on my side.

During the more recent of our nearly seventy years together, it was always Katie that wanted to write a book. She actually started two or three times. Our story, from her perspective, naturally was mostly about our family, her special accomplishments and experiences, homes we lived in, and the four kids. To us, each of them was a perfectly beautiful and special individual. Her way of recounting some of our stories was always joyful and entertaining. But our attempts to get it started in a comprehensive way, either recorded or written, always failed. Her emotions got in the way. So, I am compelled, not only by my personal motivation, but also out of loyalty to her and in recognition of how our life together was lived as one, to do the best I can and get on with this writing project.

As it happened, just a few years ago, Katie used a digital voice recorder to make a record of her memories from when we were courting and first married. That session, with my interjections, lasted for two and a half hours, but was never to be continued. Our daughter Jan has transcribed all of that recording and printed for our extended family this first chapter of what I titled *Katie's Book*. In order to include some of Katie's own words in my book, here are two extractions from her recording. The first is about the interval between my Army separation in 1945 and the start of college in early 1946. We had moved into Grandma Mersch's upstairs in Cedar Falls.

> . . . *That was just until school started from November to the first week of January. During that time we discovered that we were pregnant with Becky, so we didn't know for sure whether she was conceived in Grandma's upstairs or in Belleville, Illinois. But as soon as we found out that if she had been conceived in Belleville while you were still in the Air Force the baby would be paid for, naturally we settled on her conception being while we were still in Belleville. Becky was born in July of 1946.*
>
> *So, when we were in Grandma's upstairs I was so sick to my stomach, and Grandma insisted on me going down and helping her with the wringer washer and it was hard and so I would go down and help her and then begin throwing up. And so she'd say, "You just go on upstairs. I'll take care of this." And she did.*
>
> *It was while we were there, we had your parents and mine for dinner and we had a card table. And all we had at Grandma's upstairs was a hot plate. I was going to cook a roast. A pot roast. I had bought it and then I asked Grandma if I could cook it in her oven and she said, of course. So then I asked her how much water should I put on it and how much salt. So that was the main dish and then we had potatoes and some kind of a vegetable but all I remember was the main part of the meal. And it was pretty nice.*
>
> *At Grandma's we had a bedroom and some kind of a little room attached to the bedroom. See, Grandma rented out that*

room to school teachers when school was on and we just happened to need it and it was available. Every time you made a move in the bed the coil springs would squeak. And when Grandma would come up to the attic to get stuff she needed she would pause at the landing and say, "Yoo-hoo!"

And I remember coming down the stairs. Grandpa was the first one I saw coming down the stairs, when I said, "Grandpa! We're going to have a baby!" And they were both really happy about that, but Grandma said to my mother, "And they don't even have a home." And it was quite a while before we had a home. . . .

The second extraction from Katie's recording is about our life in the trailer parked in Maplewood Park, Illinois, throughout 1947 and early 1948.

. . . I want to talk about that trailer park. When you're pregnant and you have to go to the bathroom a lot? And there was an outdoor privy. So I would use a little plastic potty and throw it out the door in the nighttime. It wasn't terribly sanitary but I would not go out there in the nighttime. At first, you started going with me. We didn't throw it out. I think we took it out. It was a vacant lot and we had a flashlight and everything and so we took it out. It was Becky's potty. It went with Becky's potty chair.

So that was a good time for Becky and me. Because we had other friends. There were birthday parties, and there was another little girl her age that came.

Well, and then for a bath there—you used the facilities at the college —I was allowed to go twice a week to take a bath at her [the landlady's] house. In between I relied on a bar sink, about 14 inches square. And Becky had her own little pink bathtub. So we made do. And your mother came to visit us. So she wore her fox stole when she came on the train. She came all dressed up, you know. So we put an Army cot out in the kitchen, and so that's where she stayed. When we had the Army cot in the trailer it stretched through the kitchen area and just about touched our bed. And she decided to stay one more day. She was only going to

stay the weekend, and she decided to stay one more day. And I'm
positive that the day she left was the day Tommy was conceived.

From the summer of 1967 the remainder of the decade was punctuated by cross-country moves and never-to-be-forgotten events. We sold the house in Ortega Hills that had been home for seven years. The price was just under twenty thousand dollars, the same as when we bought it. For one year we lived in Montgomery, Alabama, while I attended Air War College, class of '68.

Before that move, however, I had to do something with the Shopsmith that I had bought from Walt Gardner's widow, the officer whose remains I had escorted to Arlington. It is a very large multi-functional woodworking machine that can be used, for example, as a lathe, a drill press and/or a table saw. There was a Railway Express depot right across from the main gate of the Jacksonville Naval Air Station. I built a big wooden crate around the Shopsmith and found a way to get it trucked over there. It was rail-shipped to Jim Shadle. I think he still has it.

By the way, that double-track rail line alongside Highway 17 was the main New York to Florida right-of-way. Many passenger trains went sailing by there, very close to the Ortega Hills housing where we lived. I have always known how Susan, about eleven, would take Jan, nearly seven, on fun summer outings to the swimming pool over on the naval air station. More recently it has been revealed during family "I remember when" conversations that our girls, along with neighborhood kids, would enjoy entertaining the passengers flying by on those trains.

At Maxwell Field, Montgomery, Alabama, home of the USAF Air University, I was checked out in the C-117, the twin-engine Douglas transport with a tail wheel. In the Navy it was the R4D, called the "Gooney Bird." We did cross-countries mostly to Washington to see about our next orders. I logged more than a hundred hours in that aircraft. Years later, when I worked as a civilian for the National Science Foundation, I had the opportunity to fly in the cockpit of an R4D from Barrows, Alaska, to Dead Horse, where the oil pipeline originates.

Air War College students were offered the opportunity to study and attend a weekly class in international affairs taught by a professor from George

Washington University. I took that, of course, and was awarded a GWU master of science degree in international affairs. We joined a Presbyterian Church and Susan and Jan went to school, but we never really fit in with the Deep South flavor of Montgomery. I was, however, right at home on the three 18-hole golf courses at Maxwell Field.

My next orders were to proceed to Long Beach, California, and report aboard the USS *Kearsarge*, CVS-33, as the Executive Officer. *Kearsarge* was an Essex class Aircraft Carrier that had been modified with a hurricane bow and an angled flight deck. She was built in 1944 and was most honored for service in combat operations during the Korean War.

The skipper in *Kearsarge* was Captain Creighton Cook. He had been Commander Fleet Air Wing ELEVEN during our time at Jacksonville, although not when I served on that staff. Katie knew his wife, Betty. Most of my contemporaries who were Academy graduates had a senior officer sponsor or mentor. I never knew that I had one, but, if I did, it was Captain Cook. He was responsible for assuring I acquired experience in conning the ship while mooring and unmooring both alongside and at anchor and also during underway replenishment.

I had bought a 1965 VW Bug from one of the junior officers at Jacksonville. A trailer hitch was fitted on our back bumper and we towed the Bug out to California and back. We wedged the gear shift to stay in neutral and packed it full of our belongings. The California highway patrol nailed me for towing out of the right lane. Ouch. We had to spend the night in Camarillo and go to the courthouse to pay the fine.

We found a nice house to rent in the Westminster area of Long Beach. I had to go down to the Fleet Training Center in San Diego to go through shipboard firefighting training. The reason for that became clear later, during our months at sea. As XO my most urgent duty when the ship was under way was as leader of the "Flying Wedge." That's what we called the team of about a dozen of the most experienced, highly trained firefighters in the ship. They were mostly damage controlmen.

The Air Group aboard *Kearsarge* was made up of both fixed and rotary wing antisubmarine aircraft plus utility planes, rescue helos and early warning radar planes, all of which used 115-145 octane gasoline. The weaponry included rockets, guns, bombs and torpedoes that included nuclear warheads. In addition to being an airport, that ship was a combination tank farm, arsenal and filling station. The danger of a fire was ever present and serious.

But the real extreme danger was a fire that wasn't immediately brought under control. I was about to learn the definition of "immediately."

The procedures were well established. Any indication of a fire or possible fire was to be reported using the sound-powered phones or regular telephones to the bridge by watch standers throughout the ship, or by anyone on the scene. The report had to identify the location by the number of the compartment or space. The Officer of the Deck ordered his bridge watch team to sound the alarm throughout the ship using the 1MC announcing circuit.

On hearing *"Fire! Fire! Fire!"* with the compartment number, the Flying Wedge would close in at top speed on that location. Everyone knew to get out of the way. In my two years aboard there were way too many fires. The Flying Wedge experts were always so fast that, though I tried, I rarely arrived first. A Marine orderly was assigned to me 24/7 when we were under way. For my first few months I had to insist that he have the ship absolutely memorized. His job was to clear a path and lead the way. He must not only know where a given compartment was located, but, most important, the best and fastest way to get to it.

The Captain instructed me that he would mark the time of the call *"Fire!"*. He demanded that I must contact him from the scene within one minute. Unless I could convince him that the team had the fire out or under control in that one minute, he would order the ship to General Quarters.

I recall two examples of how it actually worked. One involved the ship's incinerator located on the hangar (main) deck. It was a big enclosed firebox inside another compartment. On this occasion, quantities of trash, especially paper, had been allowed to accumulate in the compartment pending its being stuffed into the firebox. Somehow the whole mess in that compartment caught fire. The alarm was sounded, the Flying Wedge team arrived, a huge spray from a fire hose hit the fire, put it out, and I called the bridge with only about twenty seconds having passed.

The other example was a fire in the laundry down below about six decks. When I arrived at the top of the access ladder, the smoke was thick and the team chief told me the source of the fire had not been reached and it was not possible to get it under control quickly. What's more, I was hearing that one of our team was injured. I called the bridge. The ship went to General Quarters; watertight integrity was set. Damage Control Teams were manned, in position and ready. All hands were at battle stations. Within about five minutes the fire was under control; power circuits had been turned off; we were using handheld battery lanterns until additional emergency lighting was turned on; the smoke was cleared and the injured man (second-degree burns) was attended to in sick bay. After these events were reported to the bridge the all-clear was sounded. The men of the Flying Wedge saved the day.

Much of my Western Pacific 1968-69 cruise aboard *Kearsarge* involved Vietnam War operations on Yankee Station in the northern part of the South China Sea, together with escort destroyers and various resupply ships. There were in-port stretches at Subic Bay, the Philippines, in Sasebo, Japan, and a visit to Hong Kong.

One departure from that assignment took the ship farther south to participate in allied naval exercises with Australia. There were coordinated maneuvers involving ship formations with *Kearsarge* and the Australian Aircraft Carrier HMS *Melborne*, each with screening destroyers. During the execution of a formation change on a dark night, the destroyer USS *Evans* passed directly in the path of the Australian Carrier. The *Evans* was sliced completely through, midships, by the *Melbourne*. The two halves of the *Evans* passed down either side of the *Melbourne*, allowing some of the survivors to be saved with the quick reaction by the crew aboard the Carrier.

The bow half of the Evans sank quickly. The stern half stayed afloat as the frantic damage control work by the survivors was successful. The weather was calm, the sea glassy. In addition to *Melbourne* the ships closest to the scene used searchlights and lifeboats to recover survivors. The *Kearsarge* was immediately designated to receive the survivors and treat the injured.

It was about one-thirty a.m. I was awakened at the first alarm, and was able to speak with our senior medical officer. We assumed there would be many injuries, set up a triage on the hangar deck, mustered stretcher bearers, and readied our trauma and operating rooms in the sick bay.

With daybreak approaching, all of the survivors had been brought to our ship. Tragically, that was only half of the *Evans'* officers and crew. The considerable loss of life was shocking, but among the survivors there were no significant injuries. A seldom used, large space forward on the hangar deck was used to assemble the survivors. Nearly all were in whatever they were wearing at the moment of the accident. Some from the *Evans'* after-half had been able to collect a little of their belongings. *Kearsarge* was able to issue to all of them whatever clothing from supply and personal care items from the ship's store they wanted. Then we attended to preparations for a memorial service to be held on the flight deck at sunset.

Captain "Dutch" Nearman had replaced Creighton Cook as CO. When it was firmly established that the ship would be in port at Sasebo, Japan, the skipper, who knew that his wife would not be available, checked with me and asked Katie to arrange for a group of officers' wives to make the trip from Long Beach to Sasebo for a few days to be with their husbands. Katie accepted the challenge and the opportunity. She rounded up the participants, including some from the Air Group. Reservations were made and tickets bought to fly via Honolulu and Tokyo and then by train to Fukuoka and by bus to Sasebo. Becky was at home then and stayed with Susan and Jan.

At Sasebo Katie and I had a nice room in a mountaintop Japanese hotel. There was no bed, but after dinner the maid arranged the futons. The bathroom had a very large stone masonry pool used for bathing. It would hold an entire family. We were asked every day about when and how hot we wanted it filled. The view from the balcony was directly down on the harbor where the ship was at anchor. They brought our dinner there, and we wore kimonos.

Along with the ship's company and all the squadrons of the Air Group, *Kearsarge* was also home to a rear admiral and his staff. A decision was made that our ship's company and the Air Group would assemble on the flight deck one day while in port at Sasebo and stand for a formal inspection. That event and its preparation kept me away from spending precious time with Katie for two days.

Back on Yankee Station, a young officer, a lieutenant (JG), in our ship received orders to transfer to the Marine base at Da Nang in Vietnam to serve as the brig officer there. While serving there he heard that *Kearsarge* was to leave Yankee Station for a week and go to Hong Kong for a port call and then return. Our helos were back and forth to Da Nang frequently so he sent a message to me asking permission to come out to the ship, go with us to Hong Kong and return. I obtained Captain Nearman's approval, and sent word for him to come on. When he arrived aboard a few days later, he was carrying two packages: one for the skipper and one for me. Mine was a 155 mm artillery shell casing made of solid brass. It had been salvaged by Vietnamese people, hammered by hand into a vase, flared at the top. A beautiful piece of craftsmanship, it is displayed in our living room.

I remember spending many unforgettable hours up in the island or on the bridge watching flight operations. The flight deck crew wore different colored jerseys: plane handlers in green, ordnancemen in red, fuel guys in purple. The flight deck crew all wore protective helmets. The arcs of the props of the S-2 aircraft extended down to within about two feet above the deck. During flight operations the constant movement of planes, the high noise level, the 25 knots or more wind and the tight spaces demanded maximum vigilance and sure-footedness.

In the course of our 1968-69 West Pac cruise, *Kearsarge* suffered three accidents, each involving a man on the flight deck, his helmet protecting his head, but struck by a prop. In all three cases the engine was idling and the helmet saved the man from very serious or fatal injury.

With twenty-five hundred men aboard, food preparation and service was virtually constant. Every individual regularly ate his meals in and with one of the five messes: the crew's mess, the chief's mess, the officers' mess (the wardroom), the captain's mess and the flag mess. Only the crew's mess served four meals daily. The wardroom mess could hold about a hundred and fifty people at one seating. In the evening all the junior officers were served starting at five o'clock. Sharply at six p.m. the lieutenant commanders and commanders stood behind their assigned chairs with their own individual napkin holder, a brass ring with the name engraved. As president of the mess, I asked one of the chaplains or another officer to say a grace or I would say it, and then, "Please be seated."

The chief steward would bring the first entrée platter. He would be followed by other stewards with serving dishes. If we had a guest, he or she would be served first; otherwise, I was. As topics of conversation, sex, politics and religion were not allowed. When we were in port at Sasebo and on several occasions in Long Beach I was so very proud to have Katie as our wardroom guest. A wardroom steward used a chime to call the officers to dinner. When the ship was decommissioned the chime was mounted on a display board with an engraved plate and presented to me. It hangs in my study.

Near the end of our West Pac cruise there was a message to all Navy ships and stations. It contained the list of officers selected for promotion to the rank of Captain (O-6). An officer on the admiral's staff had been watching for it. He hurried down to my cabin, rushed in and shouted the news: my name and his were on the list. It was a real thrill; next to the day Katie and

I were married, this was the happiest day of my life. For me, the thrill was special because the previous year when I was first eligible, I was passed over. I don't know what my odds were for being picked this time, but I had hit the jackpot, won the lottery! I really needed Katie right there for kisses and hugs and to celebrate with me, but she was on the other side of the ocean, and there were no phones, cell or otherwise, and no email. I had always believed, and often reminded Katie and our kids, that *the best is yet to come.*

This was really our career dream come true. This was the goal toward which we had aimed all our decisions and plans. The promotion was effective immediately. Captain Nearman congratulated me and said that we would honor the Navy tradition that there is only one captain in the ship's company. So, when aboard, I kept my O-5 rank and everyone addressed me as XO. I sure as hell did wear those silver eagles and four stripes, however, whenever I went ashore.

It wasn't long before the homeward voyage began. Everyone knew that this was to be the end of the line for *Kearsarge.* She was to be decommissioned. Captain Nearman had announced to the crew and our Air Group that on departure from our last stop in the Philippines, there would be room for any of the men (there were no women in combat ships in those days) to bring home a motorcycle. Built in Japan, they were available for purchase at the Navy Exchange in Subic Bay. We found safe storage for hundreds of them. There were also my two sets of Noritake china that Katie had picked out.

Making radio contact with McMurdo.
Official U.S. Navy photograph.

The ski-equipped C-130.
Official U.S. Navy photograph.

Katie Shadle at 17.

The 1933 Plymouth. We were 17.

Punk and Katie, East Waterloo High School, 1944.

Down at the old riverbed.

In 1944 at a Cedar Heights park I carved the KS + PF heart
on the back of a bench. Leaving there on a bike,
Katie fell going down the hill and got a concussion—scary.

In 1945 at Luke Field, Arizona.
Katie took a two-day wartime train trip to be with me.

September 8, 1945. With Reverend Deerenfield in front of
the First Presbyterian Church, Waterloo, Iowa.

The wedding couple.

In 1946 Jim and Larry, Katie's brothers, rode with me in that scooter with the sidecar from East St. Louis over the bridge and through the city to the St. Louis Zoo and back.

In East St. Louis in 1946 with three-month-old Becky
in Mrs. Deem's living room. We lived in two rooms upstairs.

The house trailer, 1946.

"The facilities."

With Becky, in 1947, in front of an Ercoupe
at the Parks College flight line.

With Becky by the house trailer, 1947.

The 1941 Olds with Becky, Katie and Tom at the Perdido Bay cottage.

Wearing a parachute in front of an SNJ at Whiting Field.
Official U.S. Navy photograph.

VP-23 Crew One in 1950. CDR Lew Tamny (center),
Fowler (right), Chief Crissey (center front). This PB4Y-2 lost
its control surfaces after the hurricane eye passed.
Official U.S. Navy photograph.

Damage to PB4Y-2's the morning after.
Used with permission, H. J. "Walt" Walter, The Wind Chasers, copyright 1992.

Where we lived in Opa Locka, Florida, 1950 and 1951.

In 1952 I flew the PB4Y-2 to Waterloo.
Official U.S. Navy photograph.

WHAT'S MY LINE, INC.
NEW YORK, NEW YORK

August 18, 1955

Lt. Alfred Fowler
c/o V.W. #4
Box 11, Naval Air Station
Jacksonville, Florida

Dear Lt. Fowler:

Many thanks for being with us on WHAT'S MY LINE last
Sunday. We hope you enjoyed being on the show as much
as we enjoyed having you.

I am enclosing a check for $50 to cover your winnings.

Many thanks for your cooperation.

Cordially,

WHAT'S MY LINE

Ann Kaminsky

Ann Kaminsky

Enc.

41 EAST 57TH STREET, NEW YORK 22, NEW YORK

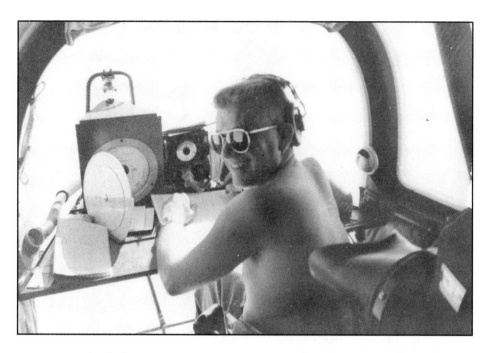

The flight aerologist station in the Plexiglas bow of the P2V.

Photograph of the ocean surface taken from low level
with the wind of 25 knots (top) and 45 knots (bottom).
Official U.S. Navy photographs.

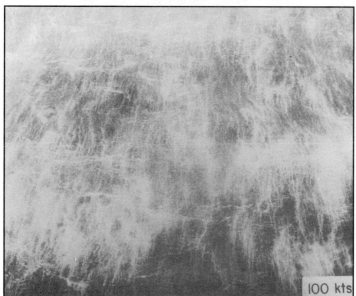

Photograph of the ocean surface taken from low level
with the wind of 70 knots (top) and 100 knots (bottom).
Official U.S. Navy photographs.

Where we lived in Metarie, Louisiana, 1957-59.

My favorite photograph of our four kids in 1958.

Katie gave me my first set of golf clubs in 1959.

Where we lived in Middletown, Rhode Island, 1959 and 1960.

At one of the Change of Command ceremonies.

Where we lived in Jacksonville, 1960 to 1967.

At the Jacksonville Officers Club.

It Was Pick-Up and Go When
OWC President Moved South

By ELAINE KENT
Times-Union Staff Writer

When a girl follows her husband from Iowa to Florida in the back of a pick-up truck, bringing with her a 2-year-old daughter and 3-month-old son, you can be pretty sure she believes in family unity.

Mrs. A. N. Fowler, 7427 Ortega Hills Drive, now plans to give similar devotion to club unity as she begins her term as president of the NAS Jacksonville Officers' Wives Club.

Besides herself and her husband, who was a member of the original hurricane-hunter squadron in this area, her family includes Becky, 17, Tom, 15, Susan, 11, and Jan, almost 7. They are serving their third tour in Jacksonville, and they lived here a total of six years.

"We have roots wherever we go," is Mrs. Fowler's solution to the problem of the traveling family.

She married her high school sweetheart in Waterloo, Iowa. "My husband was the only thing I got out of my chemistry course." Both were young, she not quite 19 and he slightly more than 19, but she has never regretted the earliness of her marriage.

Their first child was born while her husband was struggling through college, and their second arrived on graduation day when he was commissioned an ensign. Now Cmdr. Fowler, he then had the problem of getting his family and their house trailer from Iowa to Pensacola, where he was to undergo flight training.

They had a bicycle—but no automobile.

PULLING A TRAILER with a bicycle was out of the question, so Mr. Fowler hired a man who owned a car to pull the trailer. The auto also was to serve as transportation for the family.

But the car broke down shortly before the trip was to begin. Mrs. Fowler was advised by

—Times-Union Photo by Allan Walker

Mrs. Fowler: She'll Pilot Wives' Club
'We have roots wherever we go....'

her husband that she and the children would have to stay in Iowa with her parents, as the only vehicle the car's owner could offer as a substitute was a pick-up truck.

"Unless," he added hesitantly, "you want to ride in the back of the truck." Mrs. Fowler could not endure the idea of separating the family—even for a short while. "Let's do it!" she said.

"That's good," her husband replied with relief, "because I've already told him to have

the truck here at 5 o'clock."

Since then, Mrs. Fowler has come to enjoy her husband's work almost as much as he does—even the flying.

"Every wife is worried about her husband at times," she admitted, "but I have so much confidence in him, especially when he is the pilot, that I feel more at ease. Cross-country driving actually is more of a hazard than cross-country flying.

"WE ENJOY moving around," she continued, "making each place into a home. I

have put up pictures and curtains for as short a stay as for six weeks.

"One of the nicest things about being in the Navy is the close camaraderie between the wives and between the couples. You often run into people you have met years before."

Some of the places the Fowlers have seen include Newport, R. I., Monterey, Calif., New Orleans, Corpus Christie, Tex., and Miami. "We have never had an overseas tour, but we are looking forward to one eagerly."

Mrs. Fowler feels the success of the Navy life is best illustrated by the attitudes of her two oldest children. "My son wants to be a midshipman, and my daughter wants to marry one."

Mrs. Fowler's idea of a perfect evening is to go somewhere with her husband. "If we can," she said, "we go out to dinner, but if it is just before payday, we go to a drive-in movie instead. If we don't like the movie, we turn off the sound so we can talk."

Some of the other things she enjoys include sewing for her daughters, toying with the idea of writing a book and shopping. "I'm a terrible bargain hunter, I get as much of a thrill from getting a $50 dress marked down to $19 as a golfer gets from a hole in one.

"I'm a people-lover, not an animal lover," she stated. "We don't have a dog."

OF GREAT INTEREST to her within the Officers' Wives Club are the four new interest group workshops to be sponsored by the club next season. These groups will deal with arts and culture, home arts, sports and crafts.

"All leaders will be Navy wives," she explained. "The girls will take turns sharing their talents. We will feature as many activities as possible, from cake decorating to Judo."

In 1963 the *Jacksonville Times-Union* interviewed Katie.

A P2V Neptune flying by Mount Etna near Sigonella, Sicily.
Official U.S. Navy photograph.

TOM FOWLER

ALFRED FOWLER

Red-Letter Day For Dad, Son

As a Navy officer stepped up to the command of Patrol Squadron Seven at Jacksonville Naval Air Station, his son learned that he had been appointed to the U.S. Naval Academy.

The father-son career highlights occurred yesterday.

Cmdr. Alfred N. Fowler took over command of the squadron, which recently returned from a five-month deployment in the Mediterranean, at ceremonies at NAS' hangar 123.

Rear Admiral A. R. Matter, commander of Fleet Air Wings, Atlantic Fleet, was principal speaker at the change of command ceremonies.

Fowler has been the squadron's executive officer since March, 1965. He replaces Cmdr. Wycliffe D. Toole Jr., who has been ordered to the National War College in Washington as a student.

Meanwhile, Thomas James Fowler, one of four children of Cmdr. Fowler and his wife, Ka-

tie, received the academy appointment on the nomination of U.S. Rep. Charles E. Bennett of Jacksonville.

The youth will report June 29 to the academy's class of 1970 following his graduation next Wednesday at Forrest High School.

Young Fowler was also the recipient of an NROTC scholarship.

In 1966 a wonderful story appeared in the Jacksonville newspaper.

Patrol Squadron Seven SP2H, 1967.
Official U.S. Navy photograph.

On June 3, 1969, the survivors of the USS *Evans* are aboard
Kearsarge at the sunset memorial for their lost shipmates.
Official U.S. Navy photograph.

Captain Nearman in a kimono joined us for a drink
at Sasebo, Japan. *Kearsarge* can be seen through our hotel room window.

The USS *Kearsarge* CVS 33.
Official U.S. Navy photograph.

Personnel Inspection aboard *Kearsarge*.
Official U.S. Navy photograph.

Aboard *Kearsarge,* the chief steward serves python to the XO!
Official U.S. Navy photograph.

Katie pins on the captain's shoulder boards.
Official U.S. Navy photograph.

Katie with Rags at Ft. Ritchie in 1971.

Quarters C, Naval Air Station Quonset Point, Rhode Island, 1972-74.
Official U.S. Navy photograph.

In 1973, with CDR Tom Kirkpatrick, USCG,
ship operations officer. The tanker is moored alongside the ice pier.
Official U.S. Navy photograph.

The cargo ship arrives at the newly constructed
ice pier, summer of 1973-74.
Official U.S. Navy photograph.

The view to the northwest from atop Observation Hill. In the foreground are the McMurdo buildings, Winter Quarters Bay and Hut Point.

Observation Hill rises 754 feet above McMurdo Station.

Captain Alfred N. Fowler, Commander of Task Force 43 and the Naval Support Force Antarctica is welcomed by wife Katherine and daughter Janine upon his return from the five month deployment of his command to the Antarctic.

Returning home in 1974 from my last long Navy deployment.

Al and Katie being "piped over the side" between captain side boys
following the Change of Command and retirement in 1974.
Official U.S. Navy photograph.

First hole in one! May 26, 1979,
Army Navy Country Club Clubhouse, Fairfax, Virginia.

Katie with "Dame Edna" on the Warner Theatre stage in 1992.
Used with permission.

I would take special visitors by helicopter to the edge
of the sea ice where emperor penguins gathered.

Out on the Ice Shelf with Mount Erebus in the distance.

With some visitors on a nice day at the South Pole.

On the sea ice with some feathered friends.

Ruth Siple at the South Pole in 1979 with Tory Gjelsvik of Norway (right), Gordon Robin (behind Gjelsvik), and Bob Thomson of New Zealand (center). *Official U.S. Navy photograph.*

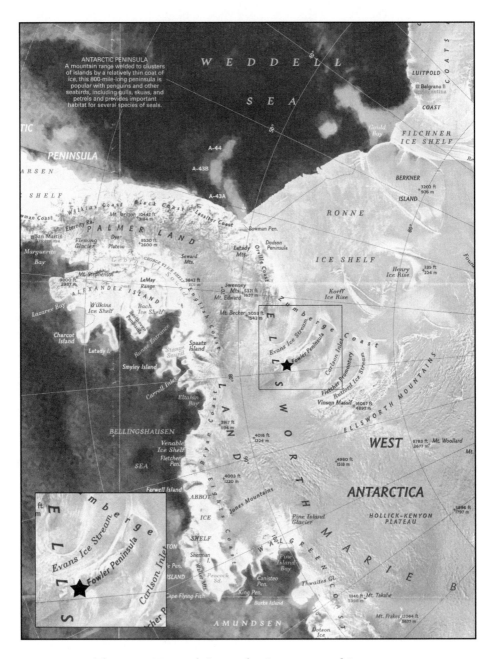

The 2002 *National Geographic Society* map of Antarctica
shows the Fowler Peninsula in West Antarctica, a star pinpointing its location.

CHAPTER IV
THE 1970S

About the middle of January 1970 we loaded the station wagon, hooked up the VW Bug, also loaded, and drove back East. Without GPS we made our way to Fort Ritchie, Maryland. My assignment was as one of the Team Leaders of the three Operations Teams at the Alternate National Military Command Center (ANMCC). It was a JCS (Joint Chiefs of Staff) tour, but not at the Pentagon. Fort Ritchie was a picturesque small Army installation in amongst the mountains on the Maryland-Pennsylvania border with family housing, PX and commissary. It also had a nine-hole golf course. The Command Center was deep inside a granite mountain just across the state line in Pennsylvania. We referred to it as "the Rock." There were about six officers and six senior enlisted men on each team. An Army bus loaded up the team on a Monday morning and delivered them from the family housing area to the Command Center in the mountain. In there, we were on watch around the clock until Friday morning. The team arriving Friday was relieved on Monday, and so forth. That meant when your team was off duty you were really off for a week with no homework, no office.

Local folklore at Fort Ritchie included a story about what happened to the crushed granite that was produced when the mountain was partly hollowed out twenty-some years earlier. The nearby forest land owned by a widow lady included a deep ravine. She accepted the hefty price offered by the government to dump the broken granite there. Then, later, she accepted an even bigger bundle from a roofing company that made good use of the granite.

The round-the-clock work at the ANMCC was only for thirteen days each month. It was a dramatic change from our previous duty in the *Kearsarge*. And, I was too senior now to do anymore proficiency flying. I loved being with Katie and the girls. But the shock of the contrast was such that I began to think about the extent to which I had either ignored my wife and children, or had deliberately left them to fend for themselves. My precious wife was remarkably resourceful and capable; she was a champion of virtue, and a perfect loving wife and mother; so much that I often fell into the easy solution of taking advantage of her. She rarely complained, but our two lives were so tightly interwoven that, when caught being selfish, I was promptly retrained to her standard of devotion and fairness.

In September of 1970 Katie and I took advantage of "space available" flying in military transports. We flew to Frankfort, Germany. We rented a car and drove to Garmisch where the U.S. military Recreation and Welfare had established hotels and other facilities. We checked into the Von Steubon Hotel to celebrate our twenty-fifth wedding anniversary. I think it is fair to say that no travel or vacation trip we ever experienced was more enjoyable. The Bavarian mountains provided the most beautiful setting. And the lodgings, the service, the food, music and dancing were the greatest. We drove around the Bavarian countryside and enjoyed every minute of it.

That space-A trip was so great—there was no delay coming or going— that a couple years later we tried it again, going to Dover, Delaware. This time, we had to wait for days. Then in Frankfort for the return trip there was no availability for several days. Finally, a civilian company flying a chartered DC-6 was rounding up all the stranded folks like us. The price was right and they agreed to take our excess baggage (a foot locker full of loot bought at the PX). That plane was full and took us to Philadelphia where we took a bus back to Dover and recovered our car.

In 1970 Tom was commissioned and graduated from the Naval Academy. To be there at that place, with all its history and tradition, and to see your son be honored as part of the graduating class is an experience of a lifetime for any parent. Katie and I were so very proud.

In the fall of 1971, I received totally unforeseen orders. We didn't expect orders for maybe another year, and what a surprise—I was to take command of an outfit home-ported in Davisville, Rhode Island, that provided support services in Antarctica, and was part of a task force with headquarters in Washington, D.C. As I described in the Introduction, this hit me cold. I scrambled to inquire and fill in the blanks by driving down to Washington. I was fairly shocked to discover that the admiral, his staff and headquarters were shutting down and moving out. In addition, the timing of my orders had been expedited so that I could make an orientation trip to Antarctica not later than Christmas.

I made the trip by way of Los Angeles, Hawaii and Samoa, then stopping for two days both ways at the U.S. staging base at the Christchurch, New Zealand, commercial airport. The flight to McMurdo Station from there is eight and a half hours in one of our ski-equipped C-130s. I stared in wide-eyed wonder through double-density Ray-Bans when the snow-and-ice-covered continent first came into view. There, in front of us, was Mount Erebus, the 13,000-foot active volcano. Like everyone else I was well outfitted in cold weather clothing and had my own personal red parachute bag full of emergency survival gear. We landed on the skiway out on an extension of the Ross Ice Shelf.

The essential introductions and my indoctrinations proceeded at a hectic pace. I had studied all of the written material I had been given, so, while the sightseeing was fantastic, the project activities and the main features of the program were pretty much as I had expected. Something about the command organization seemed way out of line, however. The flow of operations command and control occurred in the conduct of a daily radio conference between McMurdo and Christchurch. At the McMurdo end was the Commander, Antarctic Support Activities, with his department heads and the COs of the both the squadron and the Seabees. At the Christchurch end were the staff officers and sometimes the admiral. The agenda had to do with the current schedule of air, ship, station and field party operations, as well as construction and supply activities.

The conference started at ten a.m. using single frequency, two-way procedures. There was obviously a well-established discipline aimed at early adjournment. In just a few days it became clear to me that the staff in Christchurch was thoroughly devoted to local attractions such as golf, fishing, horseracing and socializing with the wonderful people of New Zealand. To that end, the size of the staff had been adjusted to include billets for several ensigns. Their purpose was to fill out a rotating schedule serving as staff duty officer at McMurdo.

Having concluded my brief orientation on the ice, I stopped by to see Admiral Leo McCuddin in his office in Christchurch. He gave me a quick summary of what was going to happen and wished me good luck. By that time, the question "Why me?" that had stuck in my mind since I had first read my orders began to be a real puzzle. I had gathered no clues from the admiral, from the orientation trip, or from a conversation with the Aviator Captain

Placement Officer at the Bureau of Naval Personnel (BUPERS). I thought about it while on that long trip home from New Zealand. I remembered an old slang expression used by Navy sailors when reacting to surprise or unwelcome orders: "I must have VD in my medical record." With that in mind, I finally figured out that since I had no sponsors in the senior ranks, my name had simply been spit out by the big BUPERS database in response to a routine requirement. I was an available-for-sea-duty aviator captain with two years' seniority and with, at least on paper, credentials in meteorology, international affairs and shipboard experience.

In April 1972, the beginning of winter in Antarctica, Katie and I with Jan moved to live in quarters at Quonset Point, Rhode Island, just adjacent to the Seabee Base at Davisville. At a change of command ceremony at Davisville I relieved Captain Gene Van Reeth as Commander Antarctic Support Activities (ASA). There were four ASA Detachments: Det Alfa was the winter-over party at McMurdo, South Pole and Palmer stations; Det Bravo was the GCA (Ground Control Approach) unit that during the off-season worked and trained at Mayport, Florida; Det Charlie was the team of aerology officers and petty officers who did the same at Norfolk; and then there was Det Delta, the year-round gang that operated the staging base at Christchurch. I quickly scheduled trips to visit my guys at Mayport and Norfolk.

I was also faced with some urgent business at the Washington Navy Yard, where the residue of the Commander U.S. Naval Support Force Antarctica, Commander Task Force 43 (CTF-43) headquarters was rapidly evaporating. The office spaces were actually being vacated. Furniture and files were disappearing. I was able to speak to the staff historian, a civilian employee about to retire. He arranged for the care of his library and for the archiving of his records. His position would itself be history.

Then I checked out the large, fully equipped photographic lab. There I found an energetic lieutenant commander staff photo officer. He was concerned about the lab there and also about the equally well-equipped labs at Christchurch and McMurdo. I told him to pick out the best of his lab equipment and I would send a truck down to haul it and him to Davisville if he would agree to transfer into my ASA organization. I was similarly able to capture the Army major who was the staff logistics and transportation expert. The staff Ship Operations Officer was U.S. Coast Guard Commander Tom Kirkpatrick. He also transferred to Davisville and proved to be my most valuable asset. Before leaving the sinking ship I managed to locate the staff Operation Officer's current files that were well organized and marked; I took possession, made good use of them and still have them. After I returned to Davisville, a work crew and a couple of trucks made a quick trip back to the Navy Yard, loaded up and returned with the photo lab, some furniture, files and so forth.

Captain Harry Swinburne, Jr., was the captain who was the outgoing admiral's Chief of Staff. He had apparently convinced someone up the line that he should be the interim Task Force Commander until a change of command could take place *in Antarctica*. In those days a "Winter Fly In," known as WINFLY, was done as soon as there was sufficient daylight out on the ice near McMurdo and the weather permitted. So, to keep everybody happy I invited Swinburne to accompany me on the WINFLY. He did. We arrived at McMurdo, assembled the troops in the mess hall and had a quick ceremony. He politely stayed out of the way for two days until all was in readiness for the northbound return trip.

A month later I returned to the ice with the season opening flight and stayed through the summer until season closing at the end of February. By coincidence, Captain Swinburne's father was one of my brother's early customers in Northeast Iowa when Bob was a stockbroker/salesman. My friend Harry Jr. retired, took over the family homestead after his dad died and became Bob's customer and good friend.

I mentioned that U.S. Coast Guard Commander Tom Kirkpatrick had agreed to make the move to Rhode Island from the defunct task force headquarters in Washington. I should explain how it happened that, as the Ship Operations Officer on my staff, he turned out to be a hero.

The small, deep water harbor at McMurdo was called Winter Quarters Bay (WQB), so named by the British early in the twentieth century. That bay was an arm of the southwest extension of the Ross Sea known as McMurdo Sound, which was covered with annual sea ice that would normally break up and move out around the first of each year. The annual resupply of the American and New Zealand Antarctic stations was done by one cargo ship and one tanker. They each needed to tie up alongside a pier or quay.

A hundred years ago, during the age of discovery, the expedition sailing or steam vessels would offload directly onto the sea ice or even the glacier front. The cargo, including coal used for fuel, would all be moved by dogsled or man-hauling to the camp site. During and since the era of Operation Deep

Freeze there has been a huge increase in the total bulk and weight of cargo. A prime example is the specially blended diesel fuel product that provides all the energy for electric generating plants, turbine engines in airplanes and helicopters, wheeled and tracked vehicles, heating systems, stationary machinery and utilities. It would be next to impossible to offload the tanker across even a mile of sea ice.

During the 1960s Operation Deep Freeze had managed to construct a wharf by driving steel girders into the earth and completing the sea wall made of timbers. The ubiquitous volcanic material was used to fill in and form the surface of the wharf.

In May of 1973 the Antarctic winter was well along. The main station at McMurdo was in the hands of the skeleton crew winter-over party. Thick sea ice had formed all over McMurdo Sound and WQB. A major powerful storm settled in that area with persistent gale force winds from the southwest. The six-foot thick sea ice broke up, was piled up raft-like and was driven across the sound and into the bay. The steel and timber wharf was demolished and completely carried away. Back in Rhode Island I was worried.

Commander Kirkpatrick devised a plan for the winter-over crew at McMurdo to build an ice pier. I gave him the green light and my ongoing full attention and support. As soon as the sea ice was thick enough bulldozers would push snow to form a berm of precise dimensions. Sea water would be pumped to a prescribed depth within the berm. With sufficiently low temperatures, and no more than moderate winds, the water would freeze and the sequence was repeated. There were many difficulties and details that had to be dealt with. The severe cold and twenty-four-hour darkness made for brutal and dangerous working conditions. It was necessary to lay a network of steel cables progressively between the layers of ice. The tidal range there was only about a foot, but the tidal motion was a problem at first. Progress was closely monitored and, by July, success was assured as long as there were no really big storms. By early October we had an ice pier some 600 feet long by 200 feet wide that was at least twenty-two feet submerged with a three-foot freeboard.

Commander Kirkpatrick had conceived and directed the project remotely by radio. By the time the sun came up vehicular bridges were in place and volcanic "top soil" had been layered onto the ice to protect it. Bollards had been frozen into it. With necessary repairs and maintenance each winter, the WQB ice pier has since been used successfully for many years.

There was another ship operations crisis in February 1974. Again it was Commander Kirkpatrick who saved the day. The tanker that year was the USNS *Maumee*. Cargo offloading had been completed and the ship was getting under way. The channel through McMurdo Sound north to the Ross Sea was ice free, but there was a thick, deep layer of sea ice fast to the shore near the entrance to WQB. The tanker was backing out, twisting the stern to starboard. With the rudder turned fully to one side, it struck the fast sea ice. The rudder was jammed and disabled. Commander Kirkpatrick worked with the ship's captain, assessed the damage and agreed on a way to center the rudder. Then chainfalls were rigged to stabilize the rudder while allowing very slight manual adjustments. The USNS *Maumee* made it back safely to just outside Littleton harbor east of Christchurch where oceangoing and harbor tugs were standing by.

During two summer seasons, '72-73 and '73-74, the Seabee Battalion that was part of TF-43 completed the construction of a new station at the South Pole. The old, original 1958 station was now buried under forty feet of snow turning to ice.

The altitude at the South Pole is about 10,000 feet, all snow and ice. The skiway, in length, is also about 10,000 feet. It is carefully kept free of drifts that accumulate wherever there is a structure or a parked tractor that sticks up to catch the wind. VXE-6, the TF-43 aircraft squadron, is constantly training its C-130 pilots in the techniques of skiway and open field operations.

One day there was a serious accident on the South Pole skiway. Thankfully no one was injured. A loaded C-130 had stalled out just as it was flaring out for landing. With its nose up and wings level in the thin air, it stalled and crash-landed tail first real hard; both wing tips dug into the snow at precisely the same time. Both wings tore from the fuselage so symmetrically and simultaneously that the wingless fuselage proceeded on its skis straight down the skiway for about a mile and a half, and finally slid to a stop. With wings and engines attached, the crew could have slowed with reverse pitch.

I arrived on the scene about three hours later. The wingless hulk had been towed off the skiway. The pilot that flew me out there had to touch down midway along the skiway to avoid the crash site. Deep furrows had been dug by the wing tips on both sides, and in the center, much farther along the track was a deep hole. Part of the cargo on the plane had been a 500-gallon rubber and fabric seal drum full of gasoline on a pallet. The rear of the plane had been torn open, the seal drum came out, was punctured, and the slow leak of gasoline ignited. The burning fuel melted the snow and ice and in three to four hours had allowed the big drum, still heavy with fuel, to melt its way down almost out of sight.

Later that day (it was most likely night, but who could tell the difference?), the accident investigation was complete and the four engines, props and chunks of broken wings were all bulldozed into the hole, preceded by four hundred pounds of dry firefighting powder. The pilot that was responsible for the loss of one of our irreplaceable ski C-130s turned out to be a Marine officer who had flown hundreds of standard wheeled C-130 hours in Vietnam, all on short runways at sea level. He wasn't ready for the South Pole and its long skiway at such high altitude. We were all thankful there were no human casualties.

I learned later that there had been one passenger aboard that flight. He was a very young seaman off the icebreaker. The ship had awarded him the trip to the pole as winner of a shipboard contest or drawing. He had been strapped in a seat up front in the cargo area and told to stay put. He evacuated with the crew thinking it had been a normal landing.

That part of the ice sheet is flowing at the rate of a foot or two per year in the general direction of the Ross Sea. So, in a few hundred thousand years, that time capsule full of engines and pieces of wings will show up at the front of the glacier as it falls into the ocean.

Here I must interrupt the storytelling to describe what it was like for me to spend those 1972 to '74 summers down on the ice at the helm of Task Force 43. The family separation was at its worst. We weren't young anymore. Three kids were thoroughly grown up and gone, and baby Jan was finishing high school. Without email or telephone the lack of family contact was a serious problem, especially for Katie.

All we had was HAM (amateur) radio. There was always a line of men waiting at the McMurdo HAM shack. There was one amateur operator in Florida who would devote many hours each day whenever the reception was clear. He would patch in the long-distance connections as long as the recipient would accept the charges. There was no privacy. It was over a single radio frequency so that the switching had to be reversed with the word *over*. Others were waiting, so most conversations were terse, impersonal and brief. A famous example was when the only message a man heard from his wife was, "Car stolen. Don't worry. Over."

Katie wrote long letters almost every day. I wrote to her about once a week. Delivery took about ten days, often longer. It was a tough tour.

The mission of providing military logistics and support for the U.S. program of year-round presence at three stations and scientific research in Antarctica had become unwieldy, wasteful and inefficient. The operation, as it had to be performed, was an annual six-month expedition that required at least a year or more of planning, positioning, training and related preparations. There was an obvious conflict on the calendar because there simply wasn't enough time when the expeditioners were also the planners.

In addition, Navy units, including those of TF-43, continually rotated their personnel so that duty tours averaged about eighteen months, rarely as much as three years. During my first summer down there, I discovered what the major issues and problems were. For example, responsible officers and senior enlisted managers had to deal with one-shot annual resupply of the consumables. As individuals they only did this for one cycle. Considering the long lead-time and the serious consequences of running out, to be safe they always doubled their order! The annual supply ship arrived at McMurdo right about Christmastime. Then for weeks there were rows and rows of material in boxes, containers and on pallets stacked outside wherever space could be found. The problem was that there were similar rows of stuff still there from last year and even from previous years.

New facilities were always under construction at McMurdo Station but sufficient warehouse space was never available. Food provisions, both keep-frozen and not-to-be-frozen were a special challenge. During my watch down there a medium-size warehouse suffered a heating failure during the winter that went unnoticed. The contents included a large amount of soft drinks and beer. There was a huge mess, as well as the loss from breakage and leakage.

Another serious problem peculiar to military support is a further fallout of the necessity for frequent rotation of people in key positions. I take you beyond the example of the pilot and his landing technique at the South Pole, and also beyond the example of double ordering the annual supply of whatever. In the urgent rush to get last year's expedition back home and have time to get next year's expedition ready to go, important lessons that had been learned the hard way were always forgotten. Men who were directly involved were transferred, often reflecting the attitude known as "FUBID." This was

Navy slang for "Fuck you, buddy, I'm detached." Their replacements were too busy to be bothered. I was very surprised to learn that the lessons learned during fourteen years of Operation Deep Freeze had not been written down anywhere. Forgotten mistakes that had proven costly in the past were being repeated with similar results.

During my second summer I tried to stir up some interest among department heads and unit leaders with the idea that we should assemble a collection of lessons learned. The idea didn't survive. It was apparent in the early 1970s that the future direction of the U.S. Antarctic Program was aimed toward the replacement of military support with one or more big civilian contractors. Now, in 2014, that transition is essentially total and has been in place for many years.

Before leaving my adventures during the 1972-74 deployments to Antarctica, I will relate a close call that involved our New Zealand neighbors. The New Zealand program used our ship and aircraft support as they occupied their Scott Base about ten miles from McMurdo. One of their research projects involved three men staying at a field camp near Cape Evans on the coast of Ross Island. The sea ice in McMurdo Sound, the body of ocean at their shore, had not yet broken up but there was a "moat" or tidal crack of open water adjoining the shore. They were biologists studying the life forms found in the shallow water not covered by ice. The sea ice pack would shift around, so they had two inflatable dinghies each with a small outboard motor.

One day the leader at Scott Base called me to say they hadn't had radio contact with the field party at Cape Evans for twenty-four hours. We agreed that one of our helos would carry their guy from Scott Base out to Cape Evans and check on the situation. Soon the report came from the helo. The camp was vacant, both dinghies were found empty, the sea ice was moving out and breaking up rapidly, and the three biologists were nowhere to be seen.

The air search was quickly launched and continued without a break for forty-eight hours. The disappearing remains of the ice pack had been searched. The shoreline had been searched. All of the party's gear, radios and cold weather clothing were at the camp. Both dinghies still contained a paddle and the emergency survival kits unopened. Neither outboard would start because of water in the fuel. I was at the air traffic control center where the search and rescue effort was being managed. A C-130 had arrived from

Christchurch with a passenger, a Chief Aerographer, who was experienced as an ice observer in the North Atlantic.

He came up to the control center for a briefing and to see the plots we had kept. The C-130 with him on board took off and went to the area for some low passes. He spotted something even though there was no sea ice apparent. The helo in the area converged on the spot and eased down to rest one ski on a fragment of ice. All three kiwis clamored aboard! They were lightly dressed, very cold, hungry, thirsty and seriously sunburned, but alive.

Their story was that as the sea ice started to move out they jumped in a dinghy. By the time they realized the engine wouldn't start they were too far away from the shore; they decided they could move quickly over the sea ice to a place where it was closer to the shore. They jumped out of the dinghy onto the ice, and failed to grab an emergency kit which contained the signaling mirror that would have saved them. Now, *there* were some very important lessons learned.

I remember that during my two years from May 1972 to May 1974 serving as boss of Operation Deep Freeze I was totally immersed in the scope and responsibility and especially the hectic tempo and flow of essential problem-solving, planning and deadlines. Each year I lived at McMurdo Station from October through March in a prefabricated building that had been used infrequently for many years as the admiral's quarters. Like in most of those buildings, the windows were painted over to allow a sleeping environment. Like all of them, mine had a vestibule where the furnace was located and where you hang your parka and leave your boots. Mine had a well-equipped kitchen, a large dining room to seat twelve, a bedroom and a bathroom with a shower. A steward would be there each morning to cook breakfast, take care of the kitchen, my laundry or anything else I needed.

I would get dressed for the outdoors and walk around town or directly to the Admin Building, which was the headquarters where "Mac Center," the air traffic control center, the main base for communication, and the weather office were located. I would speak to the duty officer at Mac Center for a rundown on the current situation and the latest revision of the daily flight schedule. Then I would sit at my desk and go through the message board. Life at McMurdo revolved around the twenty-four hour flight schedule. Nearly all the activities at McMurdo operated like the sun, around the clock. Most individuals worked on a twelve-hour cycle. Periodically, blizzard conditions provided a break when outdoor activity essentially stopped. Everyone was fed cafeteria style in one big dining room with food always being available.

At least once a week I called a meeting of all department heads plus the COs of the squadron, the Construction Battalion and the ships, if any. During my watch down there I also invited the senior National Science Foundation representative. Whenever we had senior visitors present I would put on a dinner at my quarters. The only other organized social event was the Friday night wine and cheese that my deputy, Bob Balchunas, set up. Since we had fairly regular C-130 trips back to Christchurch, he ordered the wine and cheese and had it sent down. All available officers were invited. It was held in one of the conference rooms. We would all show up in clean, even pressed, work uniforms and wear our colored dickies. The squadron wore green, CBs wore black, station and staff wore blue. NSF people and various science folks would also be our guests. Everyone seemed to have fun, as long as the wine lasted, and they made it to the mess hall for dinner in good spirits.

I really missed being part of the junior officer social group, especially with the young aviators. The members of that group down on the ice were hardworking, fun-loving young men. I remember hearing them using their own terminology: words like "neho" meaning *never ever heard of* and "whogas" meaning *who gives a shit*. Then, because radio communication was always both ways on a single frequency, they would say, "W.T.F.O.," where the *O* is for *over*. When one person in a conversation made a questionable statement another person would say it was a "wag," meaning *wild-ass guess*. Just like in most small towns everyone depended on the word-of-mouth telegraph system to keep track of the latest word. Things like, "There will be no mail call. The southbound flight was cancelled." Or, "There will be no bunny boots in the mess hall." I remember the young aviators would greet each other with, "There will be no more 'benos.'"

In the same way, naval aviators had adopted a favorite way of referring to weather conditions. Down on the ice a blizzard was "the wind blew and the shit flew." When thick clouds and overcast were moving in, if while flying, it was "in the soup" and, if on the ground, it was "stratus coming at us." The correct name for a thunderstorm cloud was cumulonimbus. Pilots called it "cumulobumpus," "thunderbumper" or "fractoscrotum."

Within the shelter of any of the stations or field camps in Antarctica one person would ask another about the nature of the weather conditions outside. The common reply would be to describe one of the two alternatives: either blizzard or no blizzard. In the case of a blizzard the reply would be

"Clear and still," meaning clear up to your ass and still snowing. If there was no blizzard, then the reply would be "Hot and dusty."

At this time, our number one son, Tom Fowler, was a junior officer naval aviator. He served in an antisubmarine helicopter squadron in San Diego. As I recall, he was available to make his way to Christchurch during the 1973-74 season. I made the arrangements and directed that Lieutenant (JG) Fowler be transported to McMurdo and be given the complete tour as my special guest. He was issued cold-weather gear and flew in our C-130s and UH-1N helicopters. He visited the South Pole Station and many other sites. Now, there was a slice of family pride that went off the charts. Today, Tom can boast that he has visited all seven continents. Come to think of it, I can, too.

Observation Hill was named by the several British expeditions early in the twentieth century. Robert F. Scott, for example, had his winter-over shelter at Hut Point on Winter Quarters Bay. Today's McMurdo Station is between that bay and Observation Hill. It is a classic inverted cone-shaped hill 754 feet in height, and perfectly situated for lookouts to keep watch to the south.

Late in the evening when the sun was in the direction of the South Pole, if the weather was clear and reasonably calm, I would climb to the top and gaze at the distant mountains, or look back over McMurdo town, or out across the ice shelf towards the skiway. Sometimes I would review the issues, people and problems or simply stare at the view and contemplate God's creation from atop Observation Hill.

When the chartered plane landed at Quonset Point in March 1974, I was the first one off and so happy to take Katie and Jan in my arms. Katie drove us to Quarters C at Quonset Point. It was so good to be home from what proved to be my last long deployment. Katie and I had speculated that a cushy overseas assignment may come next, to be our "twilight tour." But that was not to be.

Joe Fletcher, retired Air Force colonel, and a PhD scientist, was director of the Division of Polar Programs (DPP) at the National Science Foundation. He and I had worked together to get a grip on implementing the OMB Circular A-51 that eliminated the Deep Freeze line item from the DOD budget and assigned overall management and funding responsibility for the U.S. Antarctic Program to the NSF.

He called me around the first of April and asked me to meet him in

Washington. We talked as we walked the streets near the NSF headquarters at 18th and G Streets in northwest Washington. Joe wanted to retire from Civil Service, move to California and take a job with the RAND Corporation. His deputy at DPP was about to bail out also, and Joe had a plan. If I (as a retired Navy captain) would apply for his deputy's super grade position he would guarantee I would get the job. Then after a short but decent interval he would be gone and I would be directly involved with the assumption by NSF of full responsibility in Antarctica. Katie and I quickly realized that this was an opportunity not to be missed. It all happened just as Joe had laid it out. In early June there was another big change of command ceremony at Davisville. This one was also my Navy retirement. There had been between nine hundred and one thousand officers and men and a few women that made up Task Force 43 down in Antarctica. About half that number was in formation in their white uniforms at Davisville.

For two years I had reported directly to the four star admiral, Commander in Chief, U.S. Atlantic Fleet. I never met him, but his name was Admiral Ralph Cousins and I have a message he sent to me personally when I was there at McMurdo. It said that he liked the SITREPS I had been sending. Vice Admiral Douglas C. Plate, Deputy Commander in Chief, U.S. Atlantic Fleet, participated in my retirement ceremony and presented me the Legion of Merit Medal.

Katie and I drove down to Washington to look at homes to buy in the Virginia suburbs. A Realtor drove us to many listings in various areas. The last one was 9126 Glenbrook in Mantua. We bought it but found out after moving in that our dining room furniture wouldn't fit. After a few months the house three doors down at 9120 was to be listed. We bought that and sold 9126. It was much better. We fit OK but the driveway was steep and the kitchen was on the second floor. Katie heard about a house all on one floor in a great location three blocks south at 8945 Glenbrook. We fell in love with it, bought it and sold 9120. That was the summer of 1980 and it would be our last and best move.

I was already acquainted with the Division of Polar Programs offices in the NSF building in Washington. I moved into the deputy division director's office and went right to work. I was there in that job, with a few stretches as acting director, and about twenty short stays in Antarctica over a period of fourteen years. When Civil Service Reform became law I was shifted to the Senior Executive Service, Grade 4.

My main responsibility, in addition to the ongoing normal duties of the number two in the division, was to deal with and expedite the transition of management and funding of the Antarctic Program support from the Defense Department to NSF. The powers that be on the DOD side assumed that, naturally, an expeditionary project using military assets must remain one hundred percent under military control and command; the function of the NSF would be limited to paying the bills. Yet the executive orders charged NSF with the *management* as well as the funding. The way forward was the negotiating and top-level signing of an Interagency (DOD and NSF) Agreement. It took years, with the DOD stalling and impeding progress while steadily identifying more "hidden costs" that hadn't been in the original line item that was transferred.

I was frequently treated as the enemy by both sides, and generally blamed for the delay. It took about five years but the golden rule finally prevailed: "He who has the gold, rules." NSF had for a long time used a contractor in Antarctica. The requirement was simply to expand the scope, request new proposals and thereby shift more and more of the support functions to a bigger civilian contractor.

During those years I learned what the meaning was of *a billion dollars*. One year when the NSF Antarctic support contract was in competition the annual cost had grown to $100 million. There were many pieces in that overall package including manpower, construction and life support. The list goes on. I knew exactly what all the pieces and the costs were. When I stopped to think about the extension of it to a total of ten years it hit me. That tangible and understandable collection of activities, stuff and people adds up to a billion dollars.

The follow-on story here is how it happened in 1988 that I retired from my rewarding Civil Service position and took an even more rewarding half-time job at the American Geophysical Union. For that I refer all you wonderful readers (can there be any of you left?) to the previous book that I had published in 2000 entitled, *COMNAP—The National Managers in Antarctica*. Here, I will quote three paragraphs from the final chapter of that book.

> The ATCM [Antarctic Treaty Consultative Meeting] in May 1997 was in Christchurch, New Zealand. Katie accompanied me on that trip and we thoroughly enjoyed it,

including the stop-over in Hawaii on the return leg. I am very fortunate that my work in and about Antarctica has given me two satisfying careers after retirement. The very special reward is that Katie has accompanied me on so many of the trips to meetings in such interesting places. She was with me in Jackson Hole [Wyoming] in 1974, Mendoza [Argentina] in 1976, Chamonix [France] in 1978, Queenstown [New Zealand] in 1980, Bremerhaven [Germany] in 1984, San Diego in 1986, Boulder in 1987, Hobart [Australia] in 1988, Bologna [Italy] in 1991, Kyoto [Japan] in 1994, Utrecht [Netherlands] in 1996, Cambridge [England] in 1996, and Christchurch [New Zealand] in 1997.

Those trips left us with many wonderful friendships and memories of extraordinary social events and sightseeing. It was at our home in Fairfax, Virginia, however, that we enjoyed even more good times with our Antarctic friends. Katie was the chef and hostess for many memorable evenings when some of the COMNAP/SCALOP people were in Washington for a meeting. I would help with the transportation and in the scullery, and ask someone, usually Eric Chiang, to help with the bar. Those were special times that we wouldn't trade for anything.

There was another trip Katie and I made that did not include the gang from Antarctica. This one was arranged by our four children and included our brothers and sisters, their spouses and our seven grandchildren. It was to Niagara-On-The-Lake, Ontario, in September 1995 and was a celebration of our 50th wedding anniversary.

After fifty years of going to work every day I finally became unemployed in 1997. There had been weekend and after-school jobs during high school and college, a year of active duty in the Army, twenty-six years in the Navy, fourteen years of Civil Service with the National Science Foundation and nine years at the American Geophysical Union.

My active role in national and international Antarctic affairs extended from 1972 to 1997. It wasn't until about halfway through that period that protection of the Antarctic environment worked its way up to a matter of concern and finally a high priority. During my first years on the ice, it was obvious that waste management at the South Pole Station, for example, was simply to leave it in the snow where wind drift would bury it. At McMurdo Station everything went into the ocean. Early each winter, when the sea ice was thick enough in Winter Quarters Bay, a trash pile would collect on the ice. An intrepid operator in a tracked front-end loader would haul the trash out there across the tidal track to build the pile ever wider and higher. The management plan was to dump a load of contaminated fuel on the pile and set it afire. Then, the idea was that eventually the sea ice would naturally break up and the ice flow with the partly incinerated trash mountain aboard would sail out into the sound and disappear. It didn't always happen that way. The collection of trash, everything from garbage up to unwanted vehicles, would too often wind up close ashore at the bottom of the bay.

Now that I'm thinking about it, I remember well another really scary event directly involved with the lack of waste management at McMurdo. While I was "mayor" there, the one big industrial type building was the vehicle repair garage. I remember that the first time I was in that building I had noticed how the floor made of heavy timbers had become thoroughly soaked with oil and other petroleum products. I had also known that the building was too far from the shore of the bay to allow use of salt water for firefighting or for a flush toilet. Even with use of electric heat tape, they couldn't avoid a freeze-up. So, they installed an electric waste-burning toilet.

After a few years, it malfunctioned and started a fire. The flammable, tinder dry materials used in construction and the other contents of that building had rapidly ignited before the alarm was sounded. The fire department with its truck and 500 gallons of water arrived but the fire could not be controlled. One vehicle from inside and others nearby outside the garage were saved and there were no human casualties. The building and its contents were totally destroyed and what had been the floor continued to smolder for two days.

Under the broad umbrella of rules for environmental protection, I early on became an advocate for this one: The introduction of non-indigenous animal or plant species into the Antarctic Treaty area is strictly prohibited. One day I walked up the hill where the radio transmitter antenna had been built. A building there contained the transmitter equipment and was home to the technicians who operated it. While they were showing me around a scurrying critter caught my eye. It was their cat, entirely illegal and unauthorized. We had a serious talk; they knew the rules had been broken; they informed me that the cat population was exactly two, and the cats had been there in the transmitter building probably for years, but certainly, without their prior knowledge, until they arrived.

I told them that, whatever else their punishment was to be, it definitely included their attending to the disappearance of the cats. When I met later with the communications officer and his chief, they disavowed any knowledge of the cats and guaranteed the execution of the assigned punishment. In the aftermath of that illegal cat event I became aware, as did everybody else in town that was tuned in to the rumor system, that an alleged pet bird somewhere in one of the other buildings had similarly disappeared.

Several years later the national authorities of several other countries with stations in Antarctica faced the sad inevitability and removed the remaining descendents of the teams of sled dogs from the southern continent.

Katie and I enjoyed being close to the city of Washington, our nation's capital. We were invited to attend a few parties and events in the city, and would sometimes drive in for dinner at one of the restaurants. We went to the Kennedy Center and saw stage productions in both the Opera House and the Eisenhower Theatre. More than once we attended the Theatre Lab to see the *Shear Madness* play. But the most memorable stage show that we attended was at the Warner Theatre. Katie had noticed the ad in the paper about the comedy performance by Dame Edna at the Warner. I went there to the box office while on my lunch break. I expected it to be sold out, but was told by the man at the box office window after a brief delay that he had two tickets, front and center in the third row.

That evening we drove into the city, went to the theatre, took our super seats and thoroughly enjoyed the first part of the show. In the next part, Dame Edna (a hilarious male comedian from Australia who is dressed and made up to be his Edna character) set up a scene to play-act a particular situation. Dame Edna needed volunteers to play the parts. She pointed to Katie and to three other ladies near the front; asked each of them to toss one of their shoes onto the stage. Katie didn't hesitate. Off came her shoe and up it went. After a few minutes of jokes and so forth, Dame Edna said, "Come on up, girls, and we will get you into costume and give you your scripts." With one shoe on, Katie went up there. Some ushers were on hand to be sure no one stumbled.

Katie stole the show. The setup by Edna was very funny anyway, but that cute wife of mine ad-libbed her way through her part with minimum reference to the script. It was, of course, supposed to be hilarious, but Katie made it more so, and the audience howled. We couldn't get away from the lobby and the sidewalk in front of the theatre because so many people wanted to tell her how much they enjoyed her part of the skit.

More on New Zealand. Between 1972 and 1977 I was in New Zealand no fewer than twenty times. This is true, of course, because Christchurch on the South Island is the en route staging base for the U.S. Antarctic Program. I became good friends with several people who live there. I was shocked a couple of years ago to hear of the devastation to the city of Christchurch caused by an earthquake. The beautiful center of the city, the cathedral and surrounding square are so badly destroyed that reconstruction is not even being planned.

One of my kiwi friends was an elderly gentleman who was a WWII veteran of the N.Z. Air Force. His job when I knew him was to manage the welfare and recreation activities for the Americans passing through to and from Antarctica. Everyone knew him as "Smitty" and depended on him to take care of everything they needed for fishing, golf, camping and tickets to local sports and entertainment events. Smitty knew that I liked golf, found out when I was to arrive, and managed almost every time to set up and accompany me on a round at one of the local courses. He was a unique character and really fun to be with.

There was a traffic circle (they say *roundabout*) on the main street as it enters the airport. In a prominent location at that circle is the Operation Deep Freeze Officers Club. Local businessmen who seemed to have a standing invitation were almost always there to make friends with the Yanks. One man I met at the club operated a sheepskin and clothing factory and became a good friend. He was nuts about fishing and bird hunting. He and his family lived in Christchurch, but also owned a vacation home near the harbor east of the city. Then he also was part of a group that had a hunting lodge by a big saltwater lake; and he had a cottage with a boat at a big freshwater lake up in the mountains halfway across the South Island. What's more, he had positioned a house trailer on a farm along the bank of one of the mountain streams, used for spawning by the oceangoing salmon. Over the years, he arranged fishing outings at each of these places. I was always invited, and thoroughly enjoyed every one of them.

There was one of those New Zealand fishing trips so unique and fascinating that I must tell you about it. My friend met me as I arrived on the eight-and-a-half hour flight back from the ice. He said, "We are going fishing" and I should wear shoes and pants that will become soaked in brackish water; I was to be part of a working adventure that would require two full days. I assured him I was ready. There were eight of us in three cars. After a two-and-a-half hour drive near the coast, the convoy moved along the bank and then down a sort of causeway out into the big shallow lake. The lake had an inlet to the ocean that was closed then, as it was most of the time. During the hunting season that lake was visited by flocks of black swans and Canada geese. I was told that the bird shooting there was spectacular.

We arrived at the hunting lodge. We were organized in teams of two and given large gunnysacks about six feet in length—two to a team. At the water's edge we could see that the lake appeared to be very shallow and there were long strings of floats that looked like half-gallon plastic bottles. Each team was assigned to one or more of the strings.

It turned out that poachers were involved in illegally harvesting flounders from that lake. They strung the long cables, supported by the floats. Three-foot leaders were attached about every eight feet. The leaders with hooks were baited and left for several days. Our job was to start at the end, check every leader; if there was a live flounder, unhook it and put it in the sack. The water was about waist deep or slightly less and stayed that way clear across the lake, as far as we could see. The first bag became too full to lift. We dragged it through the water, crammed it full and started the other one.

On signal, all the teams worked their way back to the starting point, dragging the full sacks as far as possible. At that point I could tell that lots of advance preparations were in place. Two big freezers had been turned on, and left mostly empty, in the lodge. Outside, running water, very sharp knives, big containers and a large supply of ziplock plastic food bags were all standing by. One of the bags full of flounder was man-hauled to the work site. The others still full of live fish remained waiting in the lake. Four of the men were skilled in skinning, cleaning and beheading the fish. About a pound of fresh fillets were washed and put in each plastic bag, sealed and placed in a freezer.

Throughout the afternoon, bag after bag of live flounder was transformed into meal-sized bags of carefully washed fillets of fresh fish in the freezers. Some of us less skilled members of the team were put to work on cleanup and preparations for the dinner party that followed. New Zealand men know how to celebrate. Before the excellent dinner of fried flounder and frozen (also fried) vegetables, there was a flow of beer and whiskey that would make Niagara seem like a dribble.

In the morning there was toast, coffee and more fried flounder. The group was reorganized into three teams; the vehicles loaded to the maximum with frozen packages of flounder. They set out to the neighborhoods they knew, knocked on doors, and, by surprising friends, old and new, with a welcome gift, thus managed to distribute all of it. Now, how is that for a fun fishing trip?

As I mentioned, that fishing friend of mine operated a sheepskin factory. He produced a custom-made sheepskin coat for me. It is beautiful suede on the outside with a big collar and shearling on the inside. In addition, Katie and I have long enjoyed the sheepskin rug that fills the space between our family room and music room. It is made with the hides of four N.Z. sheep. I call it a "quarto." They call it a "fourskin."

I have sometimes mentioned some of these overseas travel destinations to various, temporarily captive, great-grandchildren. They have asked, "Which place did you like the best?"

There is, of course, no easy answer. For the grandeur of scenery it has to be Chamonix, in France, with Jackson Hole, Wyoming, a close second. For the ease of making friends with wonderful people, it is Christchurch, New Zealand. I had Katie's vote on that. We had talked about it. She visited Christchurch briefly with me early on. Then, in the spring of 1997, she was with me there for a week as I attended the Antarctic Treaty Consultative Meeting.

Many of the science, diplomatic and operations meetings were weeklong and on Thursdays there was usually a banquet. We discussed and debated which banquet was best. In terms of the venue the winner was Mendoza,

Argentina. With regard to food, it was Kyoto, Japan, and for conviviality, the best was at Hobart, Tasmania, in Australia.

As I recall that 1976 meeting in Mendoza, there are two special memories concerning food. You could have a perfectly grilled fillet of beef with accompaniments for the equivalent of two dollars. Then, with promises of a group of at least six, and if ordered at least a day ahead, you could have a card-table sized paella loaded with fresh lobster and other seafood delicacies. We did that; it was magnificent.

Another memory that pops up occurred at the Mendoza banquet. The venue was nothing less than a white marble palace built as a bodega at what was claimed to be the world's largest winery. I helped Katie find the ladies' room, which looked like a whole section of the marble palace. She was wearing an unknotted string of expensive pearls. As she came out, the string broke. The pearls bounced and rolled down the grand promenade across sleek, white marble the very same color as the pearls. She let out a squeal; diplomats and scientists joined the service staff in the bent-over melee that followed. As I recall, all of the pearls were found and returned.

One trip that Katie and I made was to London. It wasn't on official business. We were just on vacation, staying a few days in a nice London hotel. As I remember, it may have been the day of our arrival, a Saturday. I carried a leather man's purse that contained our airline tickets, traveler's checks, passports, theatre tickets and some cash. One of those black London taxis dropped us in front of our hotel. I left the purse on the back seat, and realized that after we were in the lobby.

For the rest of that day and all of the next, we struggled with the possibility we would get that purse back. The London taxi system has a lost and found. After some thirty hours, the purse had not been turned in there. The only American Express office open on Sunday was in the town of Bath. We took the train there on Sunday morning and were successful in having the travelers checks replaced. Then on Monday we spent some hours at the American Embassy and had new passports issued. As I recall, the airline made good on our return trip seats. The final chapter of the story happened about two months later. A package came in the slow boat mail. In it was my purse with everything undisturbed and accounted for.

1979 was a year in which an important American milestone was celebrated, and yet public attention was devoted to a tragic New Zealand accident. First the accident.

During that summer season in late November, a DC-10 flown by Air New Zealand with a load of high paying, mostly Japanese, passengers on an Antarctic sightseeing round-trip flight crashed into the steep slope of Mount Erebus instantly killing all two hundred seventy-five souls on board. An American helicopter flew the N.Z. Scott Base leader to view the crash site. A helicopter landing on the steep slope was not possible. Only small pieces of the tail and landing gear, but no signs of life or possible survival, were visible.

There was a story, but never officially confirmed, that was circulated at McMurdo and at Scott Base. The story had it that at the crash site, in the middle of all the death and destruction, there was a fully loaded beverage cart, standing upright with nothing broken.

I was at McMurdo Station escorting a special group of senior visitors. The site of the crash and its investigation were entirely in the hands of New Zealand authorities. The full assistance by all of the American assets had been assured. The Deep Freeze construction capabilities along with helicopter support managed to create a makeshift, very temporary, landing pad at the crash site. The N.Z. authorities with urgent Japanese input quickly declared the crash site a ceremonial "tomb" and at the same time prohibited any further attempt whatsoever toward the recovery or removal of human remains. The site was rapidly being buried in new snow. Some wreaths were laid there, and that was that.

Now, to the 1979 American celebration. It commemorated the fiftieth anniversary of the first flight over the South Pole that was accomplished by Rear Admiral Richard E. Byrd. In 1929 he had flown to the Pole and back from his camp at Little America in a Fokker tri-motor airplane. The American year-round station at the South Pole is named "Amundsen-Scott" in honor of the Norwegian and British leaders of separate expeditions that had both reached the South Pole during the 1911-12 summer. Amundsen, using dogs and skis, arrived a month earlier than Scott, man-hauling his sleds. Tragically Scott and his party died on the trip back to their base camp.

The party that I was escorting in 1979 included government officials from Norway and the United Kingdom plus Admiral Byrd's family descendants. Also in that group was my good friend Ruth Siple. She was the widow of Dr. Paul Siple. Paul had been an Eagle Scout serving as dog handler with the

Byrd expedition in the 1920s. Later Paul earned a doctorate in geology and became a leader in Antarctic earth science research.

America's plans for the International Geophysical Year 1957-58 included a year-round research station at the South Pole. Dr. Paul Siple was selected and served there as the first winter-over South Pole leader. Over the years that I knew Ruth Siple she would tell me how Paul had written many letters to her while he was at the South Pole station during that long winter night. He had described his office working and sleeping space. There were brief amateur radio contacts also. The mail was delivered to her after the first flight to the Pole.

In 1979 the old original station at the Pole had been abandoned, but was still accessible. The new station under a geodesic dome was first occupied in 1975. With a little help from the station crew I was able to lead Ruth Siple down about thirty feet on several vertical ladders into the old station. The electric lights were turned on but it was cold: minus 55°F. We went into Paul's old office. She said, for her, it was very special—the thrill of a lifetime. With minimum delay we stayed warm by climbing back up out of there.

CHAPTER V
AFTERTHOUGHTS

Now, as I dig through the memories of a lifetime, I am struck by the ways in which our world has changed in the period from the mid-twentieth to early twenty-first century. When I was growing up telephones were landline only; long distance was available but prohibitively expensive; urgent messages could be sent by telegraph, called telegrams, or cables if across the ocean. Postal service was essential for personal messages; they were normally handwritten, using what was called penmanship, with pen and ink. There was no television until well into the 1950s. Radio was essential, especially for entertainment. We listened to college football and major league baseball; also, Jack Benny, Fibber McGee and Molly, and the like.

We always had an icebox, even after the advent of electric service for lights. We remember the horse-drawn ice wagon and then the ice truck. A stiff cardboard sign was left in a window to show on the street that said *Ice* and it could be turned to indicate the size (30, 40 or 50 pounds) to be delivered. The back of the wagon or truck was always a good place for kids to get ice chips to suck on. The pan under the icebox had to be emptied of the melt water.

Coal was used for home heating. Tending the fire in the furnace was an essential skill. Properly banked for overnight, it would not require starting from scratch in the morning. A truck would deliver a ton of coal down a chute into the basement coal bin. Circulating the heat was a matter of convection (hot air rises). There was no circulating fan. The cold air return was in the floor of the room above the furnace. A container of water on top of the furnace served as the humidifier.

The movies were really big in the 1930s and '40s. There were three theaters in Waterloo. Kids could get in for a dime on Saturdays. There were always cartoons, newsreels, short subjects and the latest installment of Tom Mix. No cell phones, no video games and no TV. As I think about it, I realize that drive-in movies both appeared and disappeared during the twentieth century. Will they ever come back?

There was virtually no crime that we ever heard about. People didn't lock their doors. Little kids walked to school, and after school were given permission to go play. Cars were rarely stolen, stores rarely robbed. You never heard of houses being broken into. To use a stall in a public restroom you would need a coin to open the door. The messages written on the wall might include: "Here I sit all broken-hearted, paid a nickel and only farted."

And that also illustrates how the value of money was so different then. I remember when gasoline sold for ten cents a gallon. Men's haircuts were twenty-five cents but most parents cut their boys' hair at home to save that quarter to buy a loaf of bread *and* a quart of milk. Men who could find a job worked a long day for a dollar.

But the big change is much more than inflation in the buying power of a dollar. Ours is rapidly becoming a "cashless society." Young people today would rather have a credit card than a few tens or twenties. What's more is that the units of spending, or depletion of the plastic, are not directly equated to units of earning income from doing work.

There was plenty of alcohol and even drug abuse sixty years ago, but not in the junior high or high schools. Drunkenness to the point of alcoholism was common among the adults, and appeared to have increased following the years of prohibition and its repeal. Iowa, like many other states, was "dry." Three-point-two beer was the only alcoholic product that could be sold or legally served. There were more "beer gardens" than gas stations or food stores. Whiskey and other liquors were readily available, however, through a black market industry that apparently started with prohibition and still flourished.

Public school systems sixty or seventy years ago did not include anything about sex education or family planning and certainly nothing about sexually transmitted diseases. Young people couldn't learn much about such things from the movies or comic books. I remember that it came as a shock to me when the boys in my sixth grade class at Lowell School circulated the news that a thirteen-year-old girl in our class was pregnant. I couldn't believe it, but she disappeared and didn't go on to junior high school, so I suppose it was true.

There are other things that never change. The fundamentals of what we refer to as leadership, for example. I believe that the direct interactions that a person has with others must always be a manifestation of decency and the Golden Rule. When we think about that in terms of real life experiences, we quickly realize that the alternatives, indeed the opposite patterns of behavior, are often the common standard. It stems in part from the pressure of competition, not only in the upward levels of commercial and professional fields but also in the everyday life of regular folks and school kids.

We are all born with the gifts of human potential from our Creator including mental, emotional and physical aptitudes, the ability to learn, curiosity and common sense in discerning right from wrong. We are told that anything is possible through persistent human endeavor. Yet, all along the way, choices and decisions must be made.

I didn't fully realize until much later in life that I had witnessed the exercise of leadership (setting a decent example) in action. I refer to my exposure to my parents, Bud and Leila Fowler, Katie's parents, Ivan and Paula Shadle, my boss, Okeh Glessner, and to Chief Crissey. They were all imperfect as human beings but outstanding as leaders.

There is another hugely important change that has come about since the middle of the twentieth century. It is indelibly imprinted in my memory. Mankind is polluting the earth. My fear is that it is irreversible. When I was growing up in the Midwest it was a known fact that all the freshwater creeks, rivers and lakes were pure, or at least clean and clear. If you were thirsty you could drink the water, if you were reasonably alert to what was going on upstream. Similarly there was never any concern about the air we breathed. Now, in the twenty-first century, we have air quality warnings and ozone alerts. Freshwater lakes and streams are rarely safe for drinking and often closed to fishing and swimming because of pollution. We are told that even the oceans in some parts of the world are being spoiled or are in jeopardy of being spoiled. The production and harvesting of both fresh and saltwater seafood is being done by "farming" using various containments rather than catching the fish in the wild. The earth as a habitat, as it was available to me, is being radically changed and degraded to what will be available to my great-grandchildren.

Often I am asked whether I believe that human activities have significantly caused the warming of the global climate. Yes, I do believe that. In college I studied and began to worry about the greenhouse effect, where the heat from the sun is trapped near the earth by clouds and other ingredients of the lower atmosphere. Then, in 1972 I first visited the weather station at the South Pole. Atmospheric measurements had been recorded there continuously since 1957. At nearly two miles above sea level, that location is probably our planet's most isolated from human activity. The air samples were always taken at a place upwind and well separated from the station's buildings. The plot on a graph of the carbon dioxide contained in the air shows a historically high level and a *steady and persistent* increase. It is rapidly approaching 400 parts per million, said to be the irreversible threshold. We all should be worried about that.

Since all of you potential readers are a lot younger than me, it is left for you to contemplate the changes over the last sixty-plus years brought about by the explosion of technology. Think satellites, computers, the internet and handheld access devices. The scope of all the change is mindboggling; but it is the wild increase in the tempo of change that is the showstopper for me. I thought I was both smart and well educated; but I can't keep up.

The most important things that remain unchanged include, of course, the basic goodness of people. We are all gifted with a drive toward decency and caring and the fundamental gifts of life and love. I am therefore totally confident that the generations that follow me will be able to not only keep up, but get out in front. Our world remains in good hands. And remember, the best is yet to come.

Sitting at my desk staring at a blank page I was prompted to turn around; there on the bottom shelf of the bookcase was my personal copy of the 1919 edition of the Common Service Book of the Lutheran Church. On the cover, imprinted in gold, is my name, spelled A-l-f-o-r-d. (That spelling will be the subject of another story.) On the front flyleaf I wrote my name in pencil and "confirmed March 17, 1940—Palm Sunday—Age 13—Pastor—G.E. Melchert."

My mother, bless her heart, accepting no arguments or excuses, had insisted that Bob and I both attend confirmation classes every Saturday at the Trinity Lutheran Church. We did, and stuck with it in part because Pastor Melchert would always go with the class out to the empty lot across the street to play softball for an hour. For the next couple years, that was before our country entered the war, our mom would walk with Bob and me to attend church. My dad, wonderful in other ways, never went to church. Then, as mobilization changed everyone's way of life, we stopped going. I never again attended a Lutheran service, until I accompanied my mother to church during the last few years of her life, down in Arkansas.

While Katie and I were courting, her family's Presbyterian faith made itself known to me, but by more than church attendance. It was the personal strength of character on the part of her parents, the way they talked, conducted themselves and took care of their family of five kids. The time I spent as a grown young man with the Shadle family was an important part of my Christian education. Those unintended and unstructured lessons are with me still. We were married at the First Presbyterian Church in Waterloo. Katie's mom and dad were charter members. I was still in uniform on September 8, 1945, so Reverend Deerenfield refused to accept the five dollars I offered him.

Then we were fully occupied by college, flight training and a young family. In 1952 we attended the Navy Chapel in Jacksonville and later, in Monterey, we enrolled Becky and Tom in the Navy Chapel Sunday School. Back in Jacksonville, our skipper's wife, Ada Allen, was telling Katie that she was running the protestant Sunday school and needed help. Katie said I would gladly be a teacher. So for many weeks, whenever I wasn't flying, Ada and I operated the Sunday school. Ada played the piano, so when both classes assembled we all sang hymns. That is when Ada introduced me to an old Methodist hymn called "In the Garden." I have been singing it to myself ever since. When I arranged a funeral for my mother in 2004, I asked the choir at her Lutheran church to sing "In the Garden." They did, and I felt good about that.

Katie and I with our kids worshipped as part of Presbyterian congregations in Metarie, Louisiana, and Montgomery, Alabama. We used military chapels at Jacksonville, Monterey, Fort Ritchie, Maryland, and Quonset Point Naval Air Station in Rhode Island. After Navy retirement, we moved to Northern Virginia and attended the National Presbyterian in the District for a few weeks before we discovered Henry Baumann at Fairfax Presbyterian Church, where I reached a high point in my participation in the workings of the church serving as a member of the session from 2001 to 2004.

And now, I want to tell about my brother, Bob. Readers will recognize that my brother, Bob Fowler, my only sibling, was a salient feature and my hero during my adolescence. He also became the family embodiment of the horrors of combat in World War II. After being drafted in 1943, he went through basic infantry training and became part of the 12th Armored Infantry Division. The 12th was part of a large force being prepared for eventual invasion of Europe. Many of the infantrymen were placed on various university campuses in the interim. Bob was at Texas A&M, where he studied electrical engineering during the 1943-44 winter. In late 1944 and early 1945, the 12th AID was in combat as part of the allied forces in France and Germany.

One day Bob's company was ordered to advance toward the enemy that was dug in on the other side of a deep drainage ditch by using the foot bridges. The German machine guns aimed at the bridges opened up with devastating accuracy. Bob was shoulder to shoulder with his buddy who was directly hit and killed. Bob was seriously injured by shrapnel. He was awarded the Purple Heart. In military hospitals Bob recovered from the physical wounds in about six months. But his recovery from what is now known as post traumatic stress disorder went on for about four more years after he returned home. He then married, and he and his wife had a wonderful life. Both are gone now, leaving two wonderful daughters.

And, finally, the story on the spelling of my name: Alford versus Alfred. In 1926 my mother and dad had been married for two years. Neither one had gone to high school. They were teenagers. My brother was seventeen months old. My dad had no steady job. That would be their salvation and would come about two years later. They lived with my mother's grandmother in her home at 316 Edwards Street in Waterloo. That lady was Elizabeth Coutts, my beloved great-grandmother, "Grandma Great," that I was so very close to for twenty years.

She had lost her husband, owned her home and was the matriarch of a large collection of relatives. Her sister, Nettie, was there. Elizabeth's children included Ernest, a WWI veteran and my grandfather. He was there. Clifford, his brother, and Myrtle, his sister, were there. Reginald, another brother and his wife, Lillian, were there. Herbert, a bachelor, and my mother were Ernest's offspring. Then there was my dad, and my brother, Bob. It was a big house, but I still don't know how they all fit and I am fairly sure very few of them were bringing home regular pay. So, you can probably well imagine how it was on August 29 that I was born on Grandma Great's living room couch.

Apparently the county issued one birth certificate and the doctor's office issued another. My mother had a streak of flamboyance that expressed itself in her naming of children. Bob's middle name was Llewellyn, which he hated. She named me Alford Noel and ignored the certificate confusion. During all my school years in Waterloo, everyone in my family, and later in Katie's family, were oblivious to the first name confusion simply because my given name was never used anyway. I was known to all as Punk. My dad gave me that name when I was a toddler because he thought my shape was that of a pumpkin. My brother used it exclusively, and it stuck. All of my Iowa, Minnesota and Michigan relatives still know me as Punk. Katie never really accepted anything else, and over the years referred to me as Al only in non-family gatherings.

Anyway, my mother had heard or read the name Alford somewhere and apparently convinced the doctor that Alford was to be my name. Somebody else in the certificate business didn't get the word. When I was processed into the Army, the guy said, "Alford isn't a real name." So the Army knew me as Alfred. As years went by the Navy accepted me as Alfred, also. But, when I was thirteen my mother realized I must have a Social Security card. You guessed it; she took me there with my Alford birth certificate, her favorite one, so I have been registered with Social Security all these years as *Alford*. I discovered it just recently in 2012 when I reported Katie's passing. They issued me a new, corrected, Social Security card that says *Alfred*.

And, as it happens, a peninsula is named for me. When I was the Antarctic Task Force Commander in 1972, '73 and '74, one of the major ongoing research projects involved the measurement of the ice thickness. All of the twelve nations with science programs on the continent were actively collecting the data, but the map of the earthly terrain under the ice remained mostly blank. Then, the Americans, British, and Soviets started a coordinated plan to use long-range air operations with radio ice-sensing or echo-ranging equipment. The work progressed for at least fifteen years. Along each track flown, the height in relation to sea level of the ice surface and the height of underlying earth could be plotted. In the case of flying the ice-sensing aircraft over an ice shelf, the vertical sounding would also show the ice-ocean margin, as well as the earth below. Analysis of all the ice-sensing data made it possible to develop a complete topographic map of the earth under all that Antarctic ice.

Then, in the 1990s, satellites with sophisticated radar were able to depict the details of the surface of the ice and snow. The February 2002 issue of *National Geographic* magazine included as an insert a new National Geographic map of Antarctica. It shows the satellite imagery of the surface of the ice sheet as well as the details of coastlines that had been previously unknown. The geographic feature that was named for me is shown as the Fowler Peninsula. My name had been nominated and was used because the mapmakers of thirty-five years ago needed to put names on significant features discovered by aerial photography. Such features included raised areas that looked like humps—possibly the result of mountains entirely buried in the ice. Without any knowledge of the buried coastline, such a feature was called an "ice rise."

With that, I bring to a close this collection of fading memories from the life of a very blessed and frequently lucky naval aviator. My life, with its growing responsibility for wife and kids, had been exposed to various hazards by Army enlistment from August 1943 in World War II and by my Navy service throughout the Korean War, the Cold War and the war in Vietnam. It was obviously our good fortune that I avoided combat in all those twentieth century wars, but, with due regard for the nature of my noncombat assignments, I consider myself a survivor of those wars.

Having collected here, and after rereading, the memories of a lifetime, I can pick out, for the particular attention of my grandchildren and great-grandchildren, two lessons for life. The first is this: When flying a big multi-engine airplane very low over the ocean in a hurricane or very low over the snow and ice in the Antarctic, keep your wings level. Because when a wing tip dips into the water or into the snow the resulting cartwheel is nearly always fatal. The second lesson is especially for my young male descendants: When you find the girl or woman who is so perfect she steals your heart away, devote yourself to her for life. To assure your happiness make her happiness your goal. Together, with the enduring love you both share, anything is possible and life will be good. Never forget that when it comes to having a wonderful life, the more you give, the more you get. This lesson, while aimed at the males, is obviously applicable to everyone.

As I was looking through some of the old photo albums to find possible illustrations for the book, I found Katie's carefully assembled and preserved album containing all of the poems that I had written and given or sent to her. There are over a hundred poems in total, written by my hand, many in pencil, during the period from November 1943 through January 1945. In August 1944 I turned eighteen. A significant number of those poems, and some that I wrote in later years, are included in a companion publication, titled *A Poem From Punk*. I have spent several hours just now reading and reliving for the first time all those poems, after sixty-nine years have passed. Wow! What a profound experience. The words that I wrote on various pieces of paper and saved in Katie's album tell a story of how the spontaneous double attraction of high school sweethearts was evolving into the merging of two lives of everlasting love and devotion. For me, it is all still there and going strong.

ALFRED N. FOWLER
RETIRED U.S. NAVY CAPTAIN
& AUTHOR

As a junior officer during the 1950s, Mr. Fowler flew the Navy's version of the WWII B-24 Liberator. He was a Navy Hurricane Hunter for seven years before the days of satellites. His career as a naval aviator accumulated over 5,200 accident-free hours in the cockpit during the years of the Korean War, the Vietnam War, as well as the Cold War, though never in combat. In 1968-69 Commander Fowler served as executive officer in an aircraft carrier on Yankee Station during the Vietnam War. Subsequently he was assigned to serve in Antarctica as the Operation Deep Freeze Task Force commander. He was the first captain in that job following a series of seven admirals starting with Richard Byrd. After Navy retirement, he served as deputy division director of Polar Programs at the National Science Foundation, and following retirement from NSF, he was employed by the American Geophysical Union in Washington, D.C., where he served as the first executive secretary for the Council of Managers of National Antarctic Programs. He is the author of *COMNAP—The National Managers in Antarctica*. Captain Fowler's military awards include the Legion of Merit and the Antarctic Service medals. He lives in Fairfax, Virginia.